FINANCING POSTSECONDARY EDUCATION:

THE FEDERAL ROLE

D1364794

Proceedings of
The National Conference on the Best Ways for the
Federal Government to Help Students and Families
Finance Postsecondary Education

College of Charleston
Charleston, South Carolina
October 8-9, 1995

U.S. Department of Education
Richard W. Riley
Secretary

For sale by the U.S. Government Printing Office
Superintendent of Documents, Mail Stop: SSOP, Washington, DC 20402-9328
ISBN 0-16-048678-5

CONTENTS

Message From Richard W. Riley,
U.S. Secretary of Education

The United States is a strong world leader in higher education and provides families and communities with a better quality of life and more economic opportunities through extensive access to high quality postsecondary education. A major responsibility of the federal government through the U.S. Department of Education is to provide financial aid to help students attend postsecondary education. Approximately two-thirds of all student financial aid comes from the federal government.

Public officials and education leaders have a special obligation to explore the most effective and least costly ways to deliver better educational opportunities to our students and citizens. Because of the importance of education today, we must be good stewards of taxpayers' investments in education.

To explore the best ways for the federal government to help students and families finance postsecondary education, the U.S. Department of Education along with Senator Nancy Kassebaum and a host committee convened a unique national conference on October 8 and 9, 1995 in Charleston, South Carolina. This conference marked the 30th anniversary of the Higher Education Act and presented an unusual opportunity for discussion of bold new ideas that may steer the course of higher education policy in the future. Participants at the conference represented a broad spectrum of interests, geographic regions, political views, and perspectives, and engaged in lively discussion of pressing issues.

At this time when people are questioning whether there is a federal role in education, the conference participants, representing a wide variety of perspectives and political views, all agreed that there is an important federal role in financing postsecondary education. Every participant acknowledged that the financing of postsecondary education should be a shared responsibility of students, families, the federal government, states, and institutions. Although participants disagreed as to how student aid programs should be structured, there was general agreement that the U.S. Department of Education must assist students through well-structured and well-managed programs. As we approach time for reauthorization of the Higher Education Act, we should give careful consideration to the issues raised at this conference and to other thoughts and ideas relating to the structure of federal student financial aid programs.

In preparation for the conference, the U.S. Department of Education commissioned nine papers designed to spark discussion during the conference. These papers included several opinion papers and papers on the history and economic aspects of student aid policy, demographic and economic trends, and accountability. I found these papers to be extremely helpful in defining the issues and raising interesting -- and often provocative -- ideas to think about as we move to improve student financial aid and prepare for the next reauthorization of the Higher Education Act.

The following is a brief summary of conference discussions, the nine papers that were written for the conference, and a list of conference participants. My hope is that these materials will generate more thought among local, state, and national leaders, parents, business leaders, and the higher education community on these issues as we attempt to improve financial aid for college and will promote further dialogue and consensus building on these topics before the next reauthorization.

These materials are also available on the Office of Postsecondary Education home page, which can be found on the U.S. Department of Education's World Wide Web Internet server at the following URL address: http//www.ed.gov/offices/OPE/. Please feel free to copy and distribute the papers. If you have questions or comments on these materials please contact David A. Longanecker, Assistant Secretary for Postsecondary Education, U.S. Department of Education, 600 Independence Ave, S.W., ROB-3, Room 4082, Washington, D.C. 20202.

Summary of the National Conference on the Best Ways for the Federal Government to Help Students and Families Finance Postsecondary Education

From across America on October 8 and 9, 1995, 60 prominent local, state, and Congressional leaders, representatives from the postsecondary education community, and senior officials from the U.S. Department of Education gathered in Charleston, South Carolina, to discuss the future of financing higher education. The Honorable Richard Riley, Secretary of the U.S. Department of Education, and the Honorable Nancy Kassebaum, Chair of the Senate Committee on Labor and Human Resources, U.S. Congress, led insightful discussions focusing on the appropriate goals for federal aid to America's college students, identification of problems in the current financial aid system for postsecondary education, obstacles to change, and proposed solutions to address identified problems. Because the U.S. Department of Education provides more than two-thirds of all financial aid for college students, making it work more efficiently and effectively is very important for this nation's students and families, and for our future.

This outstanding group of leaders represented a broad spectrum of interests, political views, and geographic regions. Participants included presidents of institutions in each sector of postsecondary education, education association leaders, education policy experts, elected state officials, congressional staff, state postsecondary education agency representatives, students, trustees, representatives of the business community, and parents. These participants enthusiastically shared their visions of the future and engaged in in-depth discussion and analysis of options for financing higher education. The discussions were enriched and informed by a set of excellent papers commissioned to analyze many of the key issues in finding the best ways for the federal government to help students and families finance postsecondary education across the United States.

The conference began with remarks from Secretary Riley and Senator Kassebaum and a plenary session led by a panel of experts. Later, conference participants broke into small groups led by professional facilitators for in-depth discussions. The small group discussions focused on the following questions: What components of the federal student aid program are working well and should be retained? What should be changed? How would you change them? Each group's priorities for change were presented to the full session for general discussion.

Summary of Secretary Riley's Remarks:

Since the passage of the Higher Education Act 30 years ago, numerous accomplishments have been achieved in American education, including: increased college enrollment rates for high school graduates, higher college completion rates, and increased enrollment of women and minorities. However, because of the changing times and economy, more education and a higher standard of education are needed. College enrollments will continue to increase over the next decade, with the segments of college students who are most likely to need financial aid (undergraduates, younger students, full-time students, and low-income students) growing rapidly. As a result, the pressures on the federal financial aid system will increase.

In light of these pressures, the Secretary asked conference participants to consider and discuss the following issues:

- What is a reasonable balance of public and individual investment in higher education?

- What are the appropriate goals for the federal financial aid system?

- How can the federal government meet these goals in the best way possible?

- What is the best way to encourage and ensure accountability for federal dollars?

The Secretary reminded everyone that America's higher education system is the "jewel of the world." Therefore, we must find ways both to strengthen it and to help qualified students have access to it. The Secretary encouraged fresh thinking and bold ideas and asked the group to put aside the politics of the moment and to think ahead about the course of postsecondary education in order to better assist families and students and to build a stronger America.

Summary of Senator Kassebaum's Remarks:

The public has made it clear that they do not want business as usual. Although this conference focused on the future, Senator Kassebaum stressed that it is impossible to ignore the events of the moment or the changes that have taken place in the political landscape. There are several important similarities between government and higher education:

- Both are perceived as being set in their ways.

- Both are facing budgetary constraints.

- Both are unnecessarily costly.

- Both are being called upon to demonstrate results.

Although the purchasing power of federal aid has declined, an increase in federal or state financial aid is unlikely. Therefore, the Senator asked participants to consider how to maintain an effective system of education without additional outside resources. As college costs continue to increase, institutions must review their costs and consider how to reduce them.

The Senator expressed particular concern over the debt burden students are incurring and expressed strong support for the Work-Study program. She also called for increased attention to quality and ways to measure quality, a greater respect for learning, closer cooperation between K-12 and higher education, and reexamination of the best ways to support short-term training. She also expressed concern about the role of the states in measuring performance of training programs and the level of remedial education occurring in colleges. Finally, she stressed the importance of graduation.

Reaffirmation of the Federal Role:

At the time of the conference, the roles of local, state, and national government in education were being debated nationwide. Therefore, it was significant to note that the participants unanimously agreed that there is an appropriate role for the federal government in financing postsecondary education. They asserted that the federal government has changed the face of and strengthened higher education through the Land-Grant program, the Serviceman's Readjustment Act (GI Bill), and the Higher Education Act, and that investing in young people and adults who are continuing their formal education will continue to provide economic and social returns for both individuals and society. Many participants believed that the federal government should continue to be the principal source of student financial aid.

Social and demographic factors will increase budgetary pressures on the federal government. Over the next decade, the number of students graduating from high school will increase significantly, and these students will be more likely to have financial need than current students. At the same time, increasing numbers of adults are participating in postsecondary education, both because of their personal interest and because of public policies that encourage adult participation. Unless resources for financial aid are increased or programs are redesigned significantly, access to postsecondary education for deserving students will decrease. Participants agreed that decreasing access to postsecondary education is not the answer to balancing the federal budget. One of the small groups indicated that the federal government's commitment to access has already been eroded somewhat due to a number of factors, including: the expanded definition and population of eligible students; decline in the political will to help working low-income families; and a general resistance to change.

The Federal Work-Study program is an extremely successful program that has received too little attention. Work-Study jobs provide job experience, mentoring, and bonds to college campuses, as well as financial aid. Many participants advocated expanding this program, along with loan forgiveness and national service initiatives.

Virtually all participants thought that the federal government should move its guaranteed student loan funding entirely to Direct Loans or should sustain both the Direct Loans and Federal Family Education Loan (FFEL) programs. Many noted that institutions that participate in the Direct Loan program are able to process student applications more quickly than they were able to do under the FFEL program.

Some participants thought that the current political process should be changed to provide less regulation and more collaboration with associations, states, and institutions. It was suggested that a federal, state, and institutional commission on financial aid be established to make substantive recommendations about policies or process to the U.S. Department of Education and Congress.

Under the current system of annual appropriations, institutions cannot predict the availability of federal funds more than one year in advance. Better public understanding and support for higher education is necessary to obtain a strong federal commitment. Some participants believed that advocating for reallocation of limited funds instead of advocating for increased funding for federal aid is wrong. Others indicated that federal resources for postsecondary education are significant and are unlikely to grow in the future, particularly in the current budget environment, though more deserving students may become eligible.

Goals and Principles:

Participants agreed that clear goals for federal financial aid programs are necessary, and that tinkering with programs and policies before goals are defined is minimally useful. Accordingly, the conference began with a discussion of the appropriate goals and principles for federal financial aid programs.

Originally, the primary goal of federal financial aid was to help those that might not otherwise have had access to postsecondary education. Over time, however, the federal role has been expanded to include relieving the economic burden on middle-income students who would probably have obtained postsecondary education without federal support but with increasing personal and family sacrifice. Some participants believed that the federal government should return to its original objective of helping those with the largest need. Others noted that, when financial aid is focused more heavily on students with the lowest incomes, many middle-income and worthy students get priced out of certain colleges and universities. Others noted that stronger political support comes when middle-class students also benefit.

There was some discussion of providing merit-based financial aid in addition to, or instead of, need-based financial aid. Most participants thought that the need-based emphasis of the current system should be continued. Others argued that there should be less focus on access and more focus on student success in higher education. One of the small groups suggested providing modest merit programs for low-income college and graduate students to provide incentives for student success. Some participants believed that

6

students who do not have the aptitude for college studies or who lack the will to perform well are receiving financial aid, leading to increased costs, decreased credibility, and decreased productivity.

Several participants suggested that the federal government should create incentives for institutions and students to engage in certain behaviors. For example, the federal government could provide incentives to encourage schools to provide services to at-risk students in inner cities or could create incentives to encourage students to enter particular careers or to complete college.

Shared Responsibility:

There was near unanimous agreement that financing higher education should be a shared responsibility of students, families, the federal government, states, and institutions, and that these entities should work more closely together to be more effective. One group suggested defining the relative levels of responsibility as follows: students are the principal beneficiaries; students and families should be the principal support system; the federal government should be a safety net; states should be major supporters; and institutions should fill in the financing gaps.

Today, there is a societal expectation that the federal government will play a greater role in funding postsecondary education. Changes in the family structure, including higher divorce rates and the increasing number of single parents, have reduced the amount that parents are saving for their children's education. One participant noted that, given current financial restraints, federal and state governments are not likely to pay an increased share of college costs in the future. Therefore, the focus should be shifted to students, parents, employers, and institutions. Parents should be encouraged to save for their children's education and must be provided with realistic goals for doing so. Some participants suggested establishing tax policies and a need analysis formula that encourage saving for college.

The private sector should be encouraged to provide more scholarship money for higher education. One participant suggested that the federal government should provide monetary incentives to colleges and universities that raise private dollars for scholarships. Others suggested that tax incentives should be provided to businesses and communities that provide scholarship money.

Several participants noted that federal and state governments set their policies without working together and that they need to define clearly their respective missions to avoid overlap and conflicting policies. Some asserted that the federal government's role in financial aid should be pivotal, because each state has a different approach and many students migrate between states. Another participant, however, suggested that the federal government should provide block grants to the states for some programs.

Participants also noted that federal programs, including School-to-Work, Goals 2000, and student assistance, should be integrated better.

Restructuring:

Many participants proposed ways that federal programs could be restructured to improve the effectiveness and efficiency of the programs. The following is a summary of those proposals.

Consolidation of Programs:

Most participants believed that the federal government should continue to provide a combination of grants, loans, and work-study programs. Many participants thought that the current array of federal programs should be consolidated into one grant, one loan, and one work-study program. Consolidating programs would minimize the cost of administering the programs for the U.S. Department of Education and institutions and would reduce student confusion. There were several variations on how this consolidation should be done. Many participants stated that the funds from the Supplemental Educational Opportunity Grant (SEOG) and State Student Incentive Grant (SSIG) programs should be combined into the Pell Grant program, which would operate as the sole federal grant program. Many participants also recommended that the Pell Grant program be an entitlement program with benefits tied to inflation. Some also thought that the federal government should require institutions to maintain current levels of institutional investment for participation.

Pell Grant:

Some participants believed that grants should be "front-loaded" -- in other words, students should receive larger Pell Grants during their first two years than in other years. One group suggested developing a front-loading system in which the amount of aid would taper off over the four-year period. Others argued against front-loading, because attrition is a larger problem for college students than initial access to college programs. Some believed that front-loading would create a great incentive for economically disadvantaged students to attend two-year colleges and would harm four-year institutions, particularly private, four-year institutions.

Federal Work-Study:

One group suggested expanding the Federal Work-Study program by offering tax incentives to employers to make more work-study jobs available in the private sector. Others suggested that a greater tie should be created between work-study jobs and a student's career goals or community service and that penalties against working students in the need analysis formula should be reduced.

8

Remediation:

Although all participants believed that remediation is important and that the amount of funding for remediation should not be reduced, many participants suggested that remediation should be provided through another funding source, perhaps from high school budgets or additional federal commitments. Others suggested that remedial work should be funded through grants rather than loans, and that a federal/state cooperative program for remediation should be established. Some also indicated that remedial courses should be offered only in community colleges and not in universities.

Student Loans:

One participant proposed providing loan forgiveness to students who complete their programs and have need. Participants also suggested changing the repayment plans for student loans. Some believed that all loans should be repaid based upon the borrower's income. Others believed that students should be provided with many options for repayment including an income contingent repayment option.

Institutional Flexibility:

One participant suggested that an institutional line of credit should be established that would allow institutions to determine how to allocate financial aid between grants and loans.

Financial Aid Packaging:

Some participants believed that financial aid should be packaged over a two- or four-year period so that students can anticipate their future financial aid. One group suggested providing a debit card with a line of credit of $100,000 to each high school graduate. The debit card would provide loans, work-study, or grants depending upon the student's need. This type of system would send a strong signal to students about the availability of aid and personal responsibility for their educational choices.

Need Analysis Formula:

One group suggested that the need analysis system should be revised to better target subsidies and measure financial need. Under the current system, some middle-class and high-income families can manipulate their income to qualify for Pell Grants. Participants agreed that these grants should go to low-income students.

Simplicity:

Many participants believed that the current financial aid system is too complex. Excessive regulation increases the cost of education, and students are confused by the different programs. Some suggested that the Department of Education should simplify its applications, awards, and oversight of Higher Education Act Title IV programs. Others noted that consolidating programs would simplify the system and would reduce the amount of administrative paperwork.

Differentiation:

The current mix of federal aid programs does not adequately address the real needs of different groups of students pursuing different types of education and training for different purposes. Many participants believed that different sectors of postsecondary education should be treated differently. Some thought that the federal government should provide different incentives to different types of institutions and should not provide uniform funding and regulations to institutions regardless of their role and mission. One group suggested that the federal government should differentiate the mix of assistance and institutional accountability by program type, population served, program length, and student intent. Others suggested that different standards should be created for trade and proprietary schools.

Excessive Borrowing:

Many participants expressed concern about the increased reliance on loans by students, especially for first-time, entering students, and students in remediation programs. This phenomenon of reliance on loans is based on the premise that increased access is a benefit primarily to the individual. Some participants expressed dismay at the lack of understanding that access is a great benefit to society as well as to the individual. Encouraging low-income people to take out student loans can lead to excessive indebtedness, especially when the students do not complete their course work. The rising debt burden will create an increasing problem for many students, especially those from low-income families, with respect to access, persistence, completion, and career choice.

One group suggested reducing reliance on loans for certain groups -- low-income students, students taking remedial courses, and students enrolled in short-term training programs. Many suggested that remediation should be funded through grants rather than loans. Others suggested targeting grants to students with the greatest need and giving institutions discretion regarding whether to provide loans to students.

Others noted that the student loan volume has grown, because loans have become available to middle-income students who have not been saving for college. Some participants believed that these families could borrow money from commercial lenders.

Others, however, noted that middle-class families are a strong political force that believes federal financial aid should be available to their children.

Participants disagree as to whether lower loan limits should be established. One representative of a community college suggested that lower loan limits should apply to all students, including graduate students. She argued that society has a responsibility to provide access but cannot assume responsibility for subsidizing all forms of higher education. Others believed that access should be provided to any institution, and that a bright but low-income student should not be limited to a community college because he or she cannot afford to attend a more expensive institution. Another participant suggested limiting the amount of loans to tuition and fees.

Ties with Elementary and Secondary Education:

Many participants suggested better coordination between elementary and secondary institutions and postsecondary institutions. Many students who are not well prepared for college come from low-quality elementary and secondary institutions. Although most young people want to go to college, often their information about college opportunities is poor, especially if they are first-generation college students. Several participants noted that information must be provided to students as early as seventh and eighth grades so that students will have time to prepare themselves academically and financially for higher education.

Other participants noted that a higher priority should be placed on support services and outreach programs such as those currently funded through the TRIO programs (Student Support Services, Upward Bound, and Talent Search) and that more support should be provided for counseling and consumer information.

Credibility and Accountability:

Participants agreed that there is a need for increased accountability and credibility in postsecondary education. Participants noted sound economic and equity reasons for public support of education and the need for greater credibility in financial aid programs in order to continue strong government support. Some noted that institutions need to embrace competitive pressures calling for greater accountability and develop quantifiable and objective measures of institutional performance. Many noted that the marketplace alone is not enough to ensure accountability.

Some participants noted that the federal government is currently not able to measure the effectiveness of all institutions. There was disagreement, however, as to which measures of performance the U.S. Department of Education should consider. Some noted that the Department should not consider graduation rates, because many students leave school because of personal, financial, and family reasons rather than because of dissatisfaction with the education. Some also noted that measures of persistence, such as graduation rates, are particularly inappropriate performance measures for community colleges, where students may enroll for only a few courses. Additionally, if society invests in the most risky students, some will not succeed.

Some participants suggested that the Department of Education should continue to penalize institutions with high default rates. Some even suggested the creation of stronger penalties for institutions with high default rates. Others, however, argued that default rates are too simplistic and that measuring accountability with default rates has damaged the public perception of the system for financing higher education.

One participant suggested establishing sector-specific standards for institutional performance. A new accrediting process would be responsible for assessing educational performance with the Department of Education responsible for assessing administrative and fiscal performance.

Some participants believed that the criteria for institutional eligibility and for student readiness should be strengthened, and that aid to students should be marginally linked to institutional performance. It was also suggested that the Department should strengthen student eligibility requirements to incorporate the notion of readiness to succeed. One participant suggested adding institutional performance as a factor in determining an institution's eligibility to participate in Title IV programs.

Participants also suggested that the Department establish a better information system for consumers. This system would provide greater information about the availability of aid and the effectiveness of providers.

Conclusion:

Secretary Riley and Senator Kassebaum found these discussions to be extremely helpful and informative. Ideas raised at the conference will be considered with respect to future policy choices and will form the basis for discussions surrounding the next reauthorization of the Higher Education Act. The Senator and the Secretary hope that these issues will continue to be discussed in the higher education community and that dialogue between policy makers and those affected by federal education policy will continue.

Although many issues were left unresolved and require more thought and discussion, there were several important areas in which consensus was reached at the conference. First, participants unanimously agreed that the federal government should play a significant role in financing postsecondary education. Because of the extensive economic and social returns of postsecondary education for both individuals and society, all participants agreed that decreasing access to postsecondary education is not the answer to balancing the federal budget. Participants did not reach agreement as to the precise role of the federal government in financing postsecondary education. However, there was general agreement that the Work-Study program is highly effective and has been underemphasized, and that the Direct Loan program should be continued either as the only loan program or in combination with the FFEL program.

Second, participants agreed that financing postsecondary education is the shared responsibility of students, families, the federal government, states, and institutions, and that these entities need to work more closely together to be more effective. Because it will be difficult for federal and state governments to pay an increased share of college costs in the future, students, parents, employers and institutions must be encouraged to play larger roles. In particular, all participants agreed that parents should be encouraged to save for their children's education.

Finally, participants agreed that there is a need for increased accountability and credibility in postsecondary education in order to maintain strong government support. Participants did not agree as to how to improve accountability but expressed willingness to consider the issue further and engage in a continuing dialogue with other members of the higher education community.

The Federal Role in Financing Higher Education:
An Economic Perspective

Sandy Baum

The same fundamental question currently being hotly debated with respect to the federal role in funding the arts underlies the ongoing discussion of higher education policy. Is this a market in which the federal government should be involved in the first place? Political debates on the issue tend to ignore economic principles that could provide a solid foundation for policy. Rational discussions are frequently derailed by the fallacious assumption that interference in market processes is, by definition, inefficient and can only be justified on equity grounds. In fact, there are strong arguments in terms of both equity *and* efficiency for federal subsidies to postsecondary students.

Although we can argue about whether specific government policies will increase efficiency or make things worse, there is a broad consensus among economists of all political stripes about conditions under which the market does not lead to optimal solutions. Because several of these conditions exist in the market for higher education, the number of young people who continue their education beyond high school would be less than socially optimal in the absence of government subsidies. Although the programs currently in place for public funding of postsecondary education are not necessarily the most efficient, the level of support now provided by the federal government is minimal, at best, and is easily justified by economic analysis.

Market Failure, Efficiency, and Public Subsidy

The conclusion that the invisible hand of market forces maximizes efficiency depends on the assumption of perfect competition. There must be free entry and exit into the market and consumers and producers must have complete information. However, even in cases where the invisible hand maximizes output, there is no reason to believe that the distributional outcome of unfettered market processes will be consistent with social values.

The most common violations of the assumptions defining perfectly competitive markets involve monopoly power and collectively consumed goods and services, such as national defense. More relevant for higher education is the fact that private markets will also lead to inefficient outcomes if there are *externalities*, which exist when transactions between consumers and producers have an effect on third parties not accounted for by the market. The absence of the complete information required for efficient market operation is also a frequent source of market failure. These last two types of market failure are quite significant for higher education.

Externalities

The most common example of an externality is environmental pollution. Markets over-produce pollution because in the absence of property rights for air and water, firms do not view the destruction of these common resources as constituting a cost of production. The social cost of production exceeds the private cost of production.

If the social benefit of the consumption of a commodity is greater than the private benefit, there is a *positive* externality. The idea that there are significant positive externalities in elementary and secondary education is rarely debated. A literate citizenry is a prerequisite to the functioning of a democracy, and the skilled work force fundamental to economic development depends on universal education. The positive externalities of higher education are smaller and more elusive. But to argue that there are no externalities, one would have to accept the unlikely idea that the entire increase in productivity resulting from higher education is reflected in wages. In fact, better educated students are more likely to engage in professional activities with significant social benefits not fully compensated by the market. Even when high productivity levels are accompanied by commensurate individual financial rewards, the rest of society benefits from innovations and contributions. We are all affected not only by the level and quality of our own education but also by that of those around us, who can communicate and work more effectively if they are well-educated. Moreover, even if there is no shortage of, for example, scientists, if the best potential scientists are unable to enter the field because of financial constraints, society is poorer than it could be.

Incomplete Information

Standard examples of market failure involving incomplete information include markets for medical care, where consumers must rely on suppliers for information about the need for services and the quality of those services. In the case of higher education, there are several related problems. The consumers are generally young people. They have no experience with higher education and may underestimate its value. The very fact that the federal government is actively involved in subsidizing students to encourage college attendance is an important piece of information that may have a positive impact on choices. Their desire for immediate gratification and undervaluing of future benefits may cause young people to choose the job market (or a life of leisure) over human capital investment, despite the long-run inefficiency of this choice. The fact that in many cases students rely on someone else, such as parents, to pay for higher education also distorts the decision. Unfortunately, parents may be less willing to sacrifice for an education that will benefit their children but not themselves than they would be if they enjoyed the benefits directly.

All of these market imperfections work in the direction of underconsumption of higher education. People will underconsume because they are unwilling to pay for benefits that accrue to society at large. They will underconsume because they don't understand the benefits of higher education, they are unable to properly evaluate long-term benefits, and those who enjoy the bulk of the benefits are not usually in a position to finance the expenditure themselves. All of these factors suggest that government subsidies designed to increase participation in higher education may increase economic efficiency.

Credit Markets and Student Loans

Another market failure likely to cause underconsumption of higher education is in credit markets. There is strong evidence that some groups of borrowers have less access to private sector loans than they would in a perfect market. Many potential students without the resources to pay for higher education would suffer from this reality even without the basic fact that students generally have no collateral to back their loans because the capital in which they are investing is human capital. In addition, it is difficult to assess the risk of any individual student loan, the potential for default is considerable, and the cost of evaluating loan applicants and of administering loans in the relatively small amounts required by students would be high enough to make private loans unavailable to most needy potential students.

These circumstances support a government role in guaranteeing student loans, but they do not address the issue of whether the loans should be subsidized. The most logical federal program would separate subsidy from liquidity, targeting subsidies to those who would benefit from higher levels of education than they are likely to obtain otherwise. These would be people who have reasonable preparation but very restricted access to education.

Guaranteed unsubsidized loans are a sensible mode of finance for many students. However, the argument is flawed that contends it is reasonable for students to finance their own educations completely because the rate of return to the investment may be inadequate to pay off the loans incurred and, therefore, the investment will not be efficient. As previously discussed, students are likely to underinvest in education if they are not subsidized. In addition, even if debt burdens are manageable over the long run, they may look unmanageable in advance and deter attendance.

If we had only a simple, unsubsidized loan program, an additional factor contributing to underconsumption would be that the future return from any individual's education is uncertain. Although the characteristics of students and the type of education they are pursuing explain some of the variance in the rate of return, many other factors, frequently out of students' control, are also involved. This means that risk-averse students will be discouraged from borrowing to obtain the optimal level of education. The recent development of income-contingent repayment plans is a step in the right direction for addressing this problem.

But the real, practical problem with abandoning subsidized loans is that we would effectively do away with subsidies. A policy reform designed to separate liquidity from subsidy would be a positive step if the subsidy now incorporated into student loans were to be converted into grant aid. Given the low probability of such a scenario, the efficiency and equity

17

arguments for continued federal subsidies of college students should provide convincing arguments to maintain loan subsidies.

Equity Arguments

A Merit Good?

Currently equity arguments seem to be less politically acceptable than efficiency arguments, but it is a long-standing notion that the fundamental value of equal opportunity in our society requires that access to higher education not be limited by ability-to-pay. It is not "fair" that bright and motivated students should be unable to further their education simply because their families cannot afford to pay. This suggests that we think of higher education as a merit good -- one to which all members of society should have access. The definition of merit good is dependent on social and historical circumstances and may be controversial. But economic reality and the current structure of the labor market make it difficult to argue that access to higher education should not be a merit good in our society. Average monthly income for college graduates is almost twice that for high school graduates, and the gap is growing. The unemployment rate of college graduates is about half that of the total labor force. Denying access to higher education is tantamount to denying access to economic success.

In fact, this access argument can just as easily be based on the goal of efficiency. If students who have the potential to increase significantly their productivity by furthering their education are not given the opportunity to do so, society will possess less human capital and fewer productive resources than it could. There will be a smaller pie for all of us to divide.

Higher Education for All?

This does not mean that our goal should be for everyone to go to college. Simple laws of supply and demand suggest that college degrees will lose their economic value if they are too plentiful. The 1970s decline in the rate of return to higher education and the resulting concern over the "overeducated American" illustrated this. If everyone had higher education, it would cease to be the ticket to economic success or to any sort of prestige.

In addition, education cannot be distributed to people, it can only be made available. The unfortunate reality is that many people are unwilling or unable to take advantage of the benefits of higher education. Confusion over access to opportunity and actual participation in higher education has contributed to the problems we now face in convincing skeptics of the importance of higher education subsidies. Funding higher education will not solve our most basic social problems. In many cases, the least privileged members of society stand to gain the most from education opportunities. But we cannot expect postsecondary education to repair all of the damage done to those who have grown up in destitute or dysfunctional families and attended woefully inadequate elementary and secondary schools. Job training is critical, but pushing unprepared people into higher education programs may dilute the programs these institutions are able to offer and may lead to nothing more than debt defaults for the high-risk group.

Many people who agree with my strong support of significant public subsidies for students will not agree with this argument. But recognizing that higher education is not the right solution for everyone may help us to avoid some past mistakes. Certainly much of the opposition to current student aid programs arises from abuse by institutions not providing quality education and by students not adequately prepared to become educated.

The Distribution of Subsidies

Just as equity and efficiency are compatible goals in the decision about whether the government should be in the business of subsidizing college students, equity and efficiency considerations lead to similar conclusions about the targeting of subsidies. From an efficiency perspective, we should think about the increased social benefit that might result from subsidies to different groups of people.

The positive externality from a grant that allows an upper-middle-class student to avoid borrowing to pay for a private college is less than that from a grant that allows a young person at high risk of unemployment or permanent exclusion from the primary labor market to attend college. The social benefit from Pell Grants, which allowed talented and motivated incarcerated people to earn college degrees before being put back on the streets, may have been the greatest of all. The demise of this program and the declining real value of grants to low-income students in general provide clear evidence that politics dominate efficiency considerations in the design of federal subsidy programs.

Many proposals currently under consideration similarly reflect neglect of equity and efficiency. The current suggestion from a variety of political perspectives that we move toward substituting tax deductions for direct aid may solve political problems, but it does not solve economic problems. Tax expenditures have the same impact on the budget deficit as direct expenditures; only the political appearance differs. And the targeting of this form of subsidy on those who most need it and whose behavior is most likely to be altered in ways beneficial to society is more difficult. Any changes to current aid policies should be required to pass the test of increasing both equity and efficiency.

The Level of Federal Funding

Given the importance of government subsidy of higher education, is the magnitude of our current effort appropriate? Less than 1 percent of the federal budget is devoted to higher education. Although not all of these dollars are being used efficiently or equitably, it is difficult to imagine an effective policy requiring less funding.

Total federal aid to postsecondary students is approaching $35 billion, but about 70 percent is in the form of loans. Appropriations for federal aid reached just over $13 billion in the 1995 fiscal year. This represents an annual real rate of increase over the preceding decade of less than 1.5 percent. Even without considering the skyrocketing cost of attending college over the same period, this growth rate pales beside those of many other components of the federal budget.

If there is a clear role, both on equity grounds and on efficiency grounds, for public subsidy of higher education and if neither the proportion of the federal budget nor the rate of growth of expenditures devoted to higher education is out of control, the remaining question is whether the federal government should transfer even more of the cost of higher education to the states, which have traditionally borne most of the burden of financing postsecondary education.

Federal and State Roles

Unfortunately, the reality is that the strains on state budgets are leading to significant declines in institutional funding and direct student subsidies are also stagnating or shrinking. Because education captures a much larger portion of state budgets than of the federal budget, it is difficult to imagine an imminent reversal of this trend. The minimal role of postsecondary education in the federal budget makes it quite reasonable to maintain funding without dooming prospects for bringing the deficit under control. The federal government has a choice and if it chooses to leave the subsidies to the states, it is essentially accepting the reality that subsidies will wither away.

In any case, there are good economic arguments for a strong federal role in higher education subsidies. One criterion for judging which level of government should provide a service is the geographical distribution of benefits. When state university funding began, there was considerably less mobility within the United States than there is today. Although it is true that the direct economic benefits of an educational institution are concentrated in the surrounding area, the graduates of these institutions, even if most of them grew up in-state, are likely to be spread around the country during their working lives. Our economy is much too integrated to suggest that if some states choose not to educate their work forces, other states will not be affected. Even if income maintenance were perceived purely as a state function, the direct economic effects on the nation of this neglect would be significant.

From an equity perspective, if we believe that no American should be denied access to higher education because of inability to pay, the federal government must take responsibility for supporting this principle, not leave it to the discretion of financially strapped states.

Conclusion

Congress, the Department of Education, and the higher education community must face current dissatisfaction with both higher education institutions and student aid programs head on. Clearly, existing policies must be modified and strengthened. But eliminating student subsidies because they are not working perfectly, or in the name of deficit reduction, is irrational.

The percentage of high school graduates between the ages of 14 and 24 who have completed one or more years of college rose from 40 percent in 1960 to 66 percent in 1992. This represents considerable progress unlikely to have occurred in the absence of federal aid efforts. We should now devote more attention to questions such as why low-income and minority youth are so much less likely than others to earn college degrees. We should be attempting to solve the fundamental problems creating these disparities, not destroying programs that have created the possibility for increased access.

The current federal role in financing higher education, while flawed, is minimal and to reduce it further would be to abandon a basic principle of American society.

Sandy Baum is Professor and Chair of Economics at Skidmore College.

References

College Board. "Trends in Student Aid: 1984 to 1994." Washington, DC: The College Board, September 1994.

U.S. Department of Commerce. *Statistical Abstract of the United States, 1994.* Washington, DC: U.S. Government Printing Office, 1994.

Rethinking the Allocation of Pell Grants

David W. Breneman and Fred J. Galloway

Two facts motivate this analysis:

- in the constrained federal budget climate of recent years, appropriations for Pell Grants have stabilized at roughly $6 billion per year, and show little sign of growing; and,

- the value of the maximum Pell Grant as a percentage of college costs has shrunk from a 1975 high of 78 percent of the cost of a four-year public institution to 37 percent in 1993, and from 39 percent of the cost of a four-year private institution to 13 percent in 1993. In short, the early promise of the program as a true vehicle for access for low-income students has been lost.

Our purpose is to explore alternative ways of allocating this $6 billion to regain some of the earlier promise of the program.

Before turning to the analyses, a few words about the underlying economics of the Pell Grant program are in order. Currently, nearly 4 million students receive Pell Grants, but most grants are not for the maximum award. The amount awarded to each student is based on both income and assets, and it is further reduced by the need to bring total eligibility into line with funds appropriated--Pell Grants are not true entitlements, but are based upon annual appropriations.

While the maximum award authorized for 1995-96 is $4,100, the maximum award funded is much lower--$2,340 this year. Given the large number of recipients, it costs roughly $320 million to increase the maximum award by $100. Thus, nearly $6 billion in additional spending would be required to fund the authorized maximum award, a sum not likely to be forthcoming. Were we living in a more perfect world, we would advocate full funding for the program, maintaining the promise of access. Given the world as we find it, however, we think it imperative to examine more effective allocations of the current $6 billion in order to ensure as much access as possible with that sum.

Baseline Projections and the Current Allocation Formula

The tables that follow are simulations derived from the Pell Grant cost estimation model at the American Council on Education. This microcomputer-based model was developed by the Department of Education and provides information on the cost of various programmatic changes to the Pell Grant allocation formula.[1] In addition, the model also provides for the distribution of student awards by income level, dependency status, and institutional type. To generate cost estimates for the out years, the model uses the economic assumptions developed for the 1996 budget by the Office of Management and Budget.

Before proceeding to the various cost estimates, a brief discussion of the current allocation formula is in order. For each potential Pell Grant recipient, available income and discretionary net worth are first calculated based on the recipient's total income and total net worth, in a manner that sets aside certain sums for living expenses and other purposes.[2] In the next step, assessment rates are applied to available income and discretionary net worth to produce contributions from both sources. These contributions are then summed to produce the "expected family contribution" or EFC. Once the EFC has been determined, it is then used in separate formulas to produce two potential award levels, with the smaller of the two award levels being the one the student actually receives.[3]

To calculate the annual cost of the Pell Grant program, the total value of all these awards is then added to an administrative allowance to produce the total annual program cost. In our analysis, we use this methodology to provide baseline cost estimates for the five-year period from 1995-96 through 1999-2000 under two distinct scenarios. The first scenario assumes that the current $2,340 maximum grant is unchanged over the five-year period, while the second assumes a $2,340 maximum for 1995-96, increasing to $2,620 for the subsequent four years, as presented in the President's FY 1996 budget proposal. The results presented in Table One show that, under the first scenario, budget outlays over the five-year period total $31.05 billion, while under the second scenario, outlays total $34.75 billion.

Table One: Baseline Cost Estimates for 1995-96 to 1999-2000 (Cost in Millions)

Award Year	Scenario One $2,340 Maximum All Years	Scenario Two $2,340 Maximum 95/96 $2,620 Maximum other years
1995/96	$5,990	$5,990
1996/97	6,085	6,982
1997/98	6,209	7,125
1998/99	6,322	7,257
1999/00	6,445	7,396
5 Year Total	$31,051	$34,750

The Alternative Allocation Formulas

Seven alternative allocation formulas are considered in this paper:

1. "Frontloading" the awards, by which we mean limiting Pell Grants to first- and second-year students only;

2. Exclusion of all students attending proprietary institutions;

3. The combination of (1) and (2), i.e., frontloading plus exclusion of proprietary school students;

4. Targeting awards on lower-income students and families by raising the assessment rates on income;

5. Exclusion of students enrolled in less than one-year programs;

6. Exclusion of students enrolled in less than two-year programs; and,

7. Eliminating all awards smaller than $600.

We believe that a reasonable educational case can be made for each of these options, and that none violates either equity or efficiency criteria. In the discussion section of the paper, we evaluate each of the alternative allocation formulas in terms of overall programmatic cost as well as the distributional consequences for institutions.

Before discussing our results, a few words are in order regarding the process used to select the policy options for our analysis. For a particular programmatic change to be included, we required it to be policy-relevant and required that it could be estimated with a relatively high degree of precision. For many of the programmatic changes we considered, but rejected, failure to meet the second condition was the reason.[4] For example, reintroducing the net value of family residences into the need analysis was a potentially interesting programmatic change; however, since 1993-94, this information has not been collected on the federal student aid application. In this case, as well as others, the analysis would have required us to make an unrealistic set of distributional assumptions to estimate the cost of the proposed change.

In the case of certain options we did choose to pursue, it is important that we explicitly state the assumptions used in our analysis. For example, the savings estimates associated with the exclusion of either proprietary students, or students enrolled in less than one- and two-year programs, represent an upper bound on overall programmatic savings in that we have made no allowance for the possibility that these students might enroll in other types of institutions where they would remain eligible for Pell Grants. Analysts at both the Congressional Budget Office and the Office of Management and Budget suggest that up to 50 percent of these students might enroll elsewhere, cutting our estimates of program savings and increases in the maximum award possibly in half. However, since no direct empirical evidence exists to guide us, we present our savings estimates with this caveat.

Table Two presents the five-year cost savings associated with each of the seven options, together with the new maximum awards that would become possible if such savings were redirected to the remaining eligible students. In calculating the new maximum awards, we were constrained by both the annual outlays contained in our baseline projections, as well as the five-year cumulative outlays of $31.05 billion under the first scenario and $34.75 billion under the second scenario. As such, the entries in the table are expenditure neutral with respect to the current program and to the President's FY 96 budget proposal in that the savings generated by excluding some individuals from the program are used to increase the maximum awards for the remaining eligible population.[5]

Table Two: Five-Year Cost Savings Associated with Frontloading, Exclusion of Proprietary School Students, Income Targeting, Exclusion of Students in Less than One-and Two-Year Programs, and $600 Minimum Award Levels (Cost Savings in Millions)

Programmatic Change	Scenario One		Scenario Two	
	5 Year Cost Savings	Maximum Grant	5 Year Cost Savings	Maximum Grant
Frontloading	$8,403	$3,030	$9,475	$3,410
Exclusion of proprietary school students	5,134	2,710	5,698	3,030
Exclusion of proprietary school students with frontloading	13,327	3,720	14,940	4,180
Income targeting	3,016	2,540	3,338	2,840
Exclusion of students in less than one year programs	1,634	2,440	1,810	2,740
Exclusion of students in less than two year programs	4,383	2,650	4,848	2,960
$600 minimum award	606	2,370	545	2,650

Table Three then presents the distributional consequences of the various alternative allocation formulas, showing how the public, private, and proprietary sectors fare under the revised formulas. In this table, the relative gains and losses are shown for all three institutional sectors by comparing the percentage increase or decrease in that sector's share of total Pell Grant expenditures.[6] Given our assumption of revenue neutrality, the gains and losses, by definition, sum to zero.

Table Three: Changes in the Relative Shares of Total Pell Grant Dollars in the Public, Private, and Proprietary Sectors as a Result of the Various Programmatic Changes

Programmatic Change	Scenario One		
	Public	Private	Proprietary
Frontloading	-2.14%	-2.73%	4.87%
Exclusion of proprietary school students	13.62	3.36	-16.98
Exclusion of proprietary school students with frontloading	15.55	1.43	-16.98
Income targeting	-.26	-.21	.47
Exclusion of students in less than one year programs	3.46	.83	-4.29
Exclusion of students in less than two year programs	8.67	1.96	-10.63
$600 minimum award	-.09	-.02	.11
	Scenario Two		
	Public	Private	Proprietary
Frontloading	-2.22%	-2.67%	4.89%
Exclusion of proprietary school students	13.46	3.34	-16.80
Exclusion of proprietary school students with frontloading	15.26	1.54	-16.80
Income targeting	-.32	-.18	.50
Exclusion of students in less than one year programs	3.44	.97	4.41
Exclusion of students in less than two year programs	8.49	2.00	-10.49
$600 minimum award	-.07	-.01	.08

Notes:

a. For the 1999-2000 academic year, under Scenario One, every 1 percent change in the dollar distribution among the sectors amounts to a shift of about $65 million in Pell Grant funds.

b. For the 1999-2000 academic year, under Scenario Two, every 1 percent change in the dollar distribution among the sectors amounts to a shift of about $75 million in Pell Grant funds.

Discussion

"Frontloading" the grants to first- and second-year students provides the largest savings of any single option and, if implemented, would allow maximum grants of $3,030 or $3,410 under the two budgetary scenarios. The rationale for frontloading is that it would provide larger grant support for entering and second-year students, for whom higher education represents substantial risk and uncertainty. For those students who succeed in their first two years, much of that risk and uncertainty is diminished, and it is reasonable to expect them to borrow more heavily for the final two years. In essence, this option would reduce borrowing for first-and second-year students and increase it for third- and fourth-year students, while providing larger grant support in the first two years. Such a policy change would encourage more students to try higher education, while reducing loan defaults by students who start but do not complete a four-year degree.

From a distributional standpoint, frontloading would reallocate Pell dollars away from public and private institutions to those in the proprietary sector. In the 1995-96 award year, for example, the percentage of Pell dollars going to public colleges and universities would decline from 67 percent to almost 65 percent, while the percentage going to private colleges and universities would decline from about 17 percent to about 14 percent. In terms of actual dollars, the 5 percent increase for the proprietary sector translates into an additional $300 million Pell dollars.[7]

Exclusion of proprietary school students would allow an increase in the maximum grant to $2,710 under scenario one, or to $3,030 under scenario two, while the combination of frontloading with exclusion of proprietary school students would allow the maximum grant to rise to $3,720 or $4,180 under the two scenarios respectively. The rationale for excluding proprietary school students from the Pell Grant program is that many of these short course vocational programs might be more effectively and efficiently supported by the Labor Department through direct contracts with specific proprietary schools. To preserve our assumption of expenditure neutrality, it would be necessary to estimate the cost of these Labor Department programs, which would presumably be less than what is currently spent on proprietary school training through Pell Grants. Were that done, the effect would be to reduce the maximum Pell Grant made possible under this option.

As expected, excluding proprietary school students from Pell Grants benefits both public and private sector institutions. For example, in the 1995-96 award year, the percentage of Pell dollars going to public colleges and universities would increase from 67 percent to almost 80 percent, resulting in an additional $770 million Pell dollars. For private sector institutions, the 3 percent gain is more modest, reflecting a $200 million increase in funding.

However, when frontloading is combined with excluding proprietary school students, the nation's public colleges and universities are even better off, reflecting the disproportionately large number of students at two-year public, rather than two-year private institutions. Under this scenario, public sector institutions would see their share of Pell dollars increase in 1995-96 from 67 percent to almost 82 percent, while private sector colleges and universities would see their share rise by slightly less than 2 percent. In terms of actual dollars, public sector institutions would gain almost $900 million, while private sector institutions would gain less than $100 million.

Income targeting in the version considered for this paper assumes a 20 percent increase in the assessment rates on student and family income, and produces relatively modest savings, allowing maximum grants of either $2,540 or $2,840 under the two scenarios. The rationale for income targeting is that it concentrates grant funds on the most needy students; a number of approaches could have been chosen to achieve this objective. Under this particular option, the distributional consequences for all sectors are relatively minor, with the proprietary sector gaining less than half of a percent in overall program revenues. In terms of actual dollars, students at public sector colleges and universities would lose about $28 million in 1995-96, while those at private sector institutions would lose over $17 million.

The next two options focus on limiting eligibility to students who are enrolled in programs of at least two years duration, and which award a degree rather than a certificate of completion. These options would exclude students enrolled in less than two year programs in both the traditional and proprietary sectors but would include proprietary programs of at least two years duration. Savings are relatively small for the less than one-year exclusion, but the two-year limit would allow maximum grants of $2,650 or $2,960 under the two scenarios.

The distributional consequences of excluding students in less than one- and two-year programs, however, are more severe than those under income targeting. For the 1995-96 award year, excluding students enrolled in less than one year programs would produce a 3 percent gain for the public sector (from 67 percent to 70 percent) and a 1 percent gain for the private sector (from 17 percent to 18 percent). Under this scenario, students at proprietary schools would lose almost $250 million.

When students enrolled in less than two year programs are excluded from the eligibility formulas, public and private sector institutions continue to gain at the expense of the proprietary sector. If this programmatic change were to take effect in 1995-96, the proprietary sector would lose almost $610 million, as their share of total Pell dollars declined from 16 percent to 6 percent. The biggest winners would be students at public sector institutions, whose share would increase by 9 percent (from 67 percent to 75 percent). Students enrolled at private colleges and universities would also benefit as their share increased from 17 percent to 19 percent.

The final option, eliminating awards smaller than $600, produces modest savings and would allow maximum grants to increase only to $2,370 or $2,650 under the two scenarios. In addition, it has barely any distributional impact. For example, in the 1995-96 award year, the private sector's share of total Pell dollars remains essentially unchanged, while the proprietary school students gain one-tenth of a percent at the expense of students in the public sector. In total, the gain to students in the proprietary sector is less than $3 million.

Conclusions

Although we believe a case can be made for all seven of these options on grounds of efficiency and equity, we recognize that none would necessarily have a clear path in the policy arena. Hard choices must be made, however, and we would argue that these simulations demonstrate that, within current budgetary limits, greater access can be achieved than the current allocation formula permits.

---

1 The simulations in the paper were generated by Version 1.3, Update 96B Grant Cost Estimation Model. In this version, 240,000 sample records, stratified by dependency status and income level, were used together with 1993-94 program participation rates and 1994-95 application flow rates to produce the various cost estimates.
2 For dependent students, the calculations are also made for parental income and assets.
3 The two formulas are the entitlement rule, which subtracts the student's EFC from the maximum award level, and the traditional need-based rule, which subtracts students' EFC from their cost of education. When the maximum award level exceeds $2,400, the percent of cost rule, introduced in the 1992 Higher Education Amendments, is also used so that three potential award levels are calculated, with the lowest award being the one the student receives.
4 In addition to inclusion of the net value of the family home into the need calculations, other programmatic changes considered were limiting awards to those with a high school diploma or GED, eliminating the financial aid administrator's authority to use professional judgment, introducing tuition sensitivity into the award formula, as well as numerous variations on the frontloading theme.
5 The maximum awards presented in the table are for the 1999-2000 academic year, although little variation exists across award years for a given programmatic change.
6 As in the previous table, the percentage gains and losses presented are for the 1999-2000 academic year, although the gains and losses for the other years are very similar.
7 In calculating the distributional consequences of various programmatic changes, the baseline distribution of awards across sectors was compared to the distribution of awards that resulted from the new higher maximum award level. In this manner, the revenue neutrality of total programmatic cost was preserved.

David W. Breneman is Professor and Dean of the Curry School of Education at the University of Virginia. Fred J. Galloway is Director of Federal Policy Analysis at the American Council on Education.

Implications of Demographic Trends in Higher Education on Student Financial Aid Over the Next Ten Years

Mary J. Frase

The extent of the demand for student financial aid is very much a function of the level of college enrollment; the characteristics of the students, their families, and the institutions they attend; and college costs. This paper provides some background information about possible future trends in these factors over the next ten years, as they may relate to issues of financing college costs.

In order to understand what the future context for student financial aid is likely to be, it is first important to examine the present and how it evolved. Therefore, this paper begins with the present, then discusses the trends of the past ten years, and then turns to what seems likely to happen in the next ten years. The major findings in the paper are summarized below.

MAJOR FINDINGS

Enrollment

▸ Enrollment in higher education institutions increased about 18 percent between 1985 and 1995, despite the fact that the annual number of new high school graduates and the number of 18- to 24-year-olds were declining during the period.

▸ Two factors contributed to the continued growth in college enrollment. One was an increase in the proportion of 18- to 24-year-olds enrolled in college. The second was growth in the number of students over 35. While the proportion of the 35- to- 44-year-old age group enrolled in college was stable, there was a substantial increase in the size of that age group.

▸ College enrollment is projected to grow 6 percent between 1995 and 2005. Nearly all the increase will occur among students under 25; the annual number of high school graduates and the size of the 18- to 24-year-old age group will begin to rise as the children of babyboomers begin to reach this age.

▸ Undergraduate enrollment is predicted to increase between 1995 and 2005, and graduate and first-professional enrollments are expected to decrease slightly.

▸ Enrollment growth is expected to be greater for full-time and minority students than for part-time and white students, respectively.

31

Characteristics of recipients of student financial aid

▶ Among undergraduates, those more likely to receive some form of aid include black and Hispanic students, younger students, and full-time students.

▶ Graduate and first-professional students are equally as likely as undergraduates to receive some type of aid but much less likely to receive any federal aid.

Implications for student financial aid

▶ Although the rate of growth in the number of students will be lower between 1995 and 2005 than in the last decade, the portions of the student population that will be growing faster include those more likely to be recipients of federal student financial aid, namely, undergraduates, younger students, those attending full time, and minority students.

▶ Demand for student financial aid will also depend upon trends in college costs and family incomes. In the past decade, college costs rose faster than family incomes. If that trend continues, it would further increase the need for student financial aid.

▶ Unanticipated trends in college costs, unemployment, and the economic returns to a college education (which have been rising) could also lead to higher or lower college enrollments than have been projected.

THE PRESENT

In the fall of 1995, over 14 million students (undergraduate and graduate) were estimated to be enrolled in two- and four-year institutions of higher education, which is the highest level ever. The majority of these students are women, white, 24-years old or younger, and they attend public, 4-year institutions full time (see Table 1). In addition, there were approximately 1 million students in noncollegiate (i.e., less than two-year) institutions[1] in the fall of 1995, about half of whom were enrolled in private, for-profit (i.e. proprietary) schools. Much less information is available about enrollment levels and the characteristics of students in

---

[1] Throughout this paper, "higher education" or "institutions of higher education" generally refers to 2- and 4-year institutions. "Postsecondary education" is a more inclusive term and includes all less-than-2-year institutions (noncollegiate institutions whose highest award is less than an associate degree) as well as 2- and 4-year institutions. (A few less-than-2-year-institutions are included among the institutions of higher education.) Most of the discussion in the paper is restricted to students in institutions of higher education, because relatively little reliable data are available, especially over time, for the less-than-2-year institutions. The major exception is the discussion of student financial aid and Table 2, which include all postsecondary students.

noncollegiate institutions but, in general, such students are more likely to be women, older, black or Hispanic, attend full time, and come from low-income families than are students attending institutions of higher education.

Financing their children's college education can be a substantial challenge to many families. In 1993, the average charges for tuition, room, and board were about $5,800 for public institutions of higher education (for an in-state student) and $15,800 at a private institution. These charges represented 14 percent and 39 percent, respectively, of median family income (for families with children ages six to 17), and even higher percentages for families with lower income levels.

Student financial aid plays a major role in assisting families in paying for postsecondary education. For the average full-time, dependent undergraduate the proportion of total college costs covered by some form of financial aid -- grants, loans, work-study -- varies substantially by family income and the type of higher education institution attended, from 59 percent for students from low-income families in private, not-for-profit, four-year institutions to 6 percent for students from high-income families attending public two-year institutions in 1992-93. In general, the proportion of total costs covered by aid decreases as income levels increase and compared to students in public, four-year institutions, is higher for students in private, not-for-profit, four-year institutions and lower for students in public, two-year institutions.

About 40 percent of all postsecondary undergraduate students (full-time plus part-time) received some form of student financial aid in 1992-93, and about 30 percent received some form of federal aid -- 23 percent received federal grants and 19 percent federal loans. The likelihood of receiving aid (either any aid or federal aid) varied by student, family, and institutional characteristics (see Table 2). In general, among undergraduates, those more likely to receive some form of aid were women, blacks and Hispanics, younger students, low-income students, full-time students, those attending private institutions (especially proprietary schools), and those attending institutions with higher tuition and fees. Undergraduates attending four-year institutions were more likely to receive aid than those attending two- to three-year institutions but less likely than students at less-than-two-year schools. Graduate and first professional students were about as likely to receive some form of aid as undergraduates, but they were less likely to receive any federal aid. First professional students were more likely to receive any aid, and particularly federal aid, than graduate students.

THE PAST DECADE

Enrollments in institutions of higher education grew approximately 18 percent from 1985 to 1995 (with most of the growth occurring from 1985 to 1991).[2] This increase in enrollments

---

[2] Noncollegiate postsecondary enrollments rose 6 percent between fall 1990 and fall 1993, compared to a 4 percent increase in enrollments in institutions of higher education over the same period.

has taken place in light of the fact that the number of new high school graduates per year declined by about 8 percent over the decade. Similarly the number of 18-24 year-olds, considered the traditional college-age population, declined by about 12 percent between 1985 and 1995. Enrollment continued to increase for two major reasons: college enrollment rates (i.e. the proportion of the age group enrolled in college) for 18- to 24-year-olds increased and the size of the age group 35 to 44 increased. Enrollment rates for those over 24 did not change, but the number of students over 35 increased considerably because the number of 35- to 44-year-olds increased as a result of the aging of the babyboom generation. As a result of these trends, the proportion of college students who were 35 or older increased between 1985 and 1995.

There were other changes worth noting in the composition of college students in the last ten years (see Table 1). Two of the most noticeable were increases in the proportion of college students who were women and in the proportion of minority students. The number of female students increased by 25 percent over the decade compared to 10 percent for men. The higher proportion of women reflects both that women are now more likely than men to enroll in college in the fall immediately following high school graduation and that college enrollment rates among those 25 and older are higher for women than for men. The number and proportion of Asian and Hispanic students have grown considerably in recent years.

Other changes in the college student population in the past decade included a slight increase in the proportion of students attending two-year institutions and the proportion of part-time students. Older students and those attending two-year institutions are more likely to attend part time, and the increases in the proportion of two-year and older students may have contributed to the increase in the proportion of part-time students between 1985 and 1995.

The proportion of high school graduates going on to college in the fall immediately following their graduation has been rising, from about 53 percent for 1983 high school graduates to about 62 percent for 1993 graduates, and this occurred among graduates from all family income levels. Although the gap in college attendance among students from low and high income families generally has not closed (50 and 79 percent, respectively, for 1993 graduates), the proportion of low-income high school graduates going immediately to college after high school is double what it was twenty years ago.

Another important trend, and one that may be contributing to the trends in enrollment, involves the economic returns to attending and completing college. Those who have completed college earn considerably more than those who have attended some college, and both groups of college-educated workers earn more than workers of the same age who did not continue their education after high school. The relative earnings advantage associated with completing college has increased over the past two decades (as has the earnings advantage for women, but not for men, of attending some college). Furthermore, the earnings advantages for attending some college and for college completion are greater for women than for men. (In 1993, among women workers ages 25 to 34, those who had completed college had median annual earnings 99 percent higher than those with only a high school education, whereas, for

34

men, the advantage for college graduates over high school graduates was 57 percent.) The growth in the earnings advantage of those with some college or for college graduates relative to high school graduates may have contributed to the increasing enrollment rates among the traditional college-age population. The higher earnings advantage for women may be a factor in the higher enrollment rates for women than for men.

While the returns to education have been rising, the cost of attending college has also been rising -- faster than inflation and faster than family incomes. Tuition, room, and board rose 42 percent at public institutions of higher education and 68 percent at private institutions between 1980 and 1993, after taking inflation into account. Tuition, room, and board at public institutions as a percentage of median family income (for families with children six to 17) rose from 10 to 14 percent (and from 22 to 39 percent for private institutions over the same period). The increases in college costs relative to income were even greater for low-income families.

PROJECTED TRENDS FOR THE NEXT TEN YEARS

Higher education enrollment will continue to increase over the next ten years, but at a slower rate, about 6 percent from 1995 to 2005.[3] Nearly all the growth in enrollment will occur in the number students under the age of 25. As the children of the babyboomers begin to graduate from high school, the number of new graduates will increase (22 percent between 1995 and 2005) as will the size of the 18- to 24-year-old population (11 percent increase over the same period). On the other hand, the population 25 to 29 and 30 to 34 will decrease (7 and 15 percent, respectively) and those 35 to 44 will increase slightly (2 percent). The result will be a nearly stable number of students 25 and older and a decline in the proportion of such students. (A decline in the number of students 25 to 34 will be offset by an increase in the number of students 35 and older.)

Some of the recent trends in the characteristics of students are likely to continue in the next decade, some will be reversed, and in other areas there will be stability. For example, the number of women students will grow less than the number of men over the next decade (see Table 1). While the proportion of students attending public institutions will be stable, the proportion attending full time and who are undergraduates will increase, reflecting the increase in younger students, who are more likely to attend full time. The number of graduate students

---

[3] The estimates of changes in higher education enrollments between 1995 and 2005 reflect the middle alternative of enrollment projections prepared by the National Center for Education Statistics (NCES). These projections are based on the middle-level population estimates, prepared by the Bureau of the Census, and assume some increase in college enrollment rates for 18- to 24-year-olds and generally stable enrollment rates for those 25 and older. If those enrollment rate assumptions do not prove to be accurate, then enrollment levels could be substantially different from the projected levels.

and of first-professional students is projected to be slightly lower in 2005 than in 1995. Similarly, nearly all the growth in students between 1995 and 2005 is projected to be in full-time students, with relatively little increase in the number of part-time students.

In light of the underlying trends in the population, it is likely that the proportion of minority students will also increase in the next decade. The proportion of the 18- to 44-year-old population that is white, non-Hispanic will decline from 72 percent in 1995 to 67 percent in 2005, as the white population in that age range will decline about 8 percent and the minority population will increase 28 percent. Among 18- to 24-year-olds (where most of the population growth among 18- to 44-year-olds will occur in the next decade and the age group with the highest college enrollment rates), the white population will grow by 6 percent compared to 21 percent for minorities. Among minorities, the rate of population growth will be much greater for Asians and Hispanics than for blacks (e.g., increases in the number of 18- to 24-year-olds of 27 and 41 percent for Hispanics and Asians, respectively, compared to a 12 percent increase for blacks between 1995 and 2005). Given that college enrollment rates for minorities have historically been lower than for whites, it is unlikely that the change in the racial/ethnic composition of college students will be as great as in the population as a whole. Nevertheless, it still seems very likely that the trend of the past decade of increasing proportions of minority students will continue, particularly in terms of Hispanic and Asian students.

IMPLICATIONS FOR STUDENT FINANCIAL AID FOR THE NEXT DECADE

The segments of the college student population that will be growing (or growing faster) in the next decade are ones which, in the past, have been more likely to receive student financial aid, particularly federal aid. As noted above, younger students, undergraduates, full-time students and minority students are more likely to receive assistance than others. All these segments of the college student population will be growing, both in absolute numbers, and as a proportion of all students. Furthermore, while the growth in college enrollments in the next decade will be slower than in the last one, it will continue, and is likely to be greater than in the last few years with an upturn in the number of high school graduates beginning in 1996. Thus, the need for student financial aid will continue to expand.

However, changes in the number of students and their characteristics are only part of the context in terms of need for student financial assistance. Trends in college costs and family incomes will also be important. The extent of increases in tuition/fees will depend on a variety of factors, including trends in public funding for higher education (which has been declining as a percentage of all revenues for institutions of higher education) and whether institutions can realize productivity increases. Trends in family income, relative both to inflation and college costs, will also be important. If family incomes grow at a slower pace than college costs, the need for aid will be much higher than if family incomes increase at a faster rate or at the same rate as college costs. Changes in the distribution of family incomes (i.e., what happens to the poverty rate and to the size of the gap between rich and poor families) would also affect the pressures on families trying to finance college educations for their children. Thus, while the projected college enrollment trends suggest a greater demand for student financial aid in the next decade, the size of that increased demand will depend on a variety of additional factors (which in turn could affect enrollment trends as well).

Mary Frase is the Senior Technical Adviser in the Data Development and Longitudinal Studies Group, National Center for Education Statistics, in the U.S. Department of Education. Prior to joining NCES in 1985, she was a faculty member at Teachers College, Columbia University and worked as an independent consultant advising state and local governments and conducting research in the areas of education policy, education finance, and state-local finance.

Table 1. Characteristics of Students in Higher Education and Growth in Numbers of Students: 1985, 1995, and 2005

Characteristic	Percent of all students			Percent change in number of students	
	1985[1]	1995[2] (Estimated)	2005 (Projected)	1985-1995[1,2] (Estimated)	1995-2005[2] (Projected)
Total	100	100	100	18	6
Gender					
Men	48	44	45	10	9
Women	52	56	55	25	4
Level					
Undergraduate	87	86	87	17	7
Graduate	11	12	11	26	-1
First professional	2	2	2	6	-3
Attendance status					
Full-time	58	56	57	14	9
Part-time	42	44	43	23	2
Control of institution					
Public	77	78	78	19	6
Private	23	22	22	13	6
Type of institution					
2-year	37	38	39	23	6
4-year	63	62	61	15	6
Age					
Under 25	58	56	59	15	16
25-34	26	25	21	13	-8
Over 35	15	20	20	55	10
Race/ethnicity[3]					
White	82	77	--	8	--
Black	9	10	--	31	--
Hispanic	4	7	--	85	--
Asian/Pacific Islander	3	5	--	86	--
American Indian/ Alaskan Native	1	1	--	46	--

-- Not available.

[1] 1984 for race/ethnicity.

[2] 1993 for race/ethnicity and age.

[3] Percentages are based on U.S. residents and citizens only. Nonresident aliens are excluded.

Note: Percentages may not add to 100 percent due to rounding.

Source: U.S. Department of Education, National Center for Education Statistics, Projections of Education Statistics to 2005 (NCES 95-169), and Digest of Education Statistics 1995 (NCES 95-029).

Table 2. Receipt of student financial aid by postsecondary students, 1992-93

Student characteristics	Percent receiving:				Average aid per aided student			
	Any aid	Federal aid			Any aid	Federal aid		
		Total	Grant	Loan		Total	Grant	Loan
				Undergraduates				
Total	41	31	23	19	$4,200	$3,600	$1,700	$3,200
Gender								
Men	39	28	19	18	4,400	3,800	1,700	3,300
Women	43	33	25	20	4,000	3,400	1,700	3,100
Race/ethnicity								
White, nonHispanic	39	28	19	19	4,200	3,700	1,600	3,200
Black	54	46	38	26	4,100	3,400	1,700	2,900
Hispanic	43	36	31	14	3,600	2,100	1,800	3,100
Asian/Pacific Islander	31	25	19	15	5,100	3,600	1,800	3,200
American Indian/ Alaskan Native	48	34	29	15	3,600	3,000	1,700	3,000
Age (as of 12/31/92)								
23 and younger	46	35	23	23	4,700	3,700	1,700	3,000
24-29	41	34	27	20	3,800	3,600	1,700	3,600
30-39	38	27	22	14	3,300	3,400	1,700	3,600
40 or more	27	16	13	8	2,900	3,200	1,600	3,600
Income quartile/independent students								
Lowest	72	66	63	34	4,200	3,600	1,900	3,300
Middle two	36	26	20	15	3,200	3,300	1,400	3,600
Highest	20	8	2	7	2,600	3,700	1,300	3,900
Parental income quartile/dependent students								
Lowest	68	63	56	36	4,900	3,600	1,800	2,800
Middle two	38	26	10	20	5,000	3,700	1,200	2,900
Highest	29	14	1	11	4,800	4,000	1,300	3,100
Attendance status								
Full-time, full-year	58	45	29	31	5,500	4,200	2,000	3,300
Full-time, part-year	56	48	37	28	3,500	3,100	1,500	2,800
Part-time, full-year	32	22	17	12	3,100	3,000	1,500	3,200
Part-time, part-year	23	15	12	7	2,200	2,600	1,200	3,000
Control of institution								
Public	34	25	19	14	3,100	3,100	1,600	2,900
Private, not-for-profit	60	44	26	34	7,000	4,500	2,000	3,500
Private, for-profit	72	68	50	46	4,200	4,000	1,700	3,500

Table 2. Receipt of student financial aid by postsecondary students, 1992-93 (continued)

Student characteristics	Percent receiving:				Average aid per aided student			
	Any aid	Federal aid			Any aid	Federal aid		
		Total	Grant	Loan		Total	Grant	Loan
Undergraduates								
Level of institution								
Less than 2-year	61	57	47	31	3,500	3,400	1,700	3,300
2- to 3-year	30	22	18	9	2,500	2,600	1,400	2,900
4-year	50	38	24	28	5,300	4,100	1,900	3,300
Type of institution								
Public								
Less-than-2-year	22	17	16	1	1,500	1,400	1,200	2,900
2-year	27	18	16	6	2,100	2,200	1,400	2,600
4-year								
Nondoctoral granting	45	36	27	22	3,700	3,400	1,700	2,800
Doctoral granting	46	34	21	26	4,300	4,100	1,800	3,200
Private, not-for-profit								
Less-than-4-year	54	43	34	25	3,500	3,200	1,700	2,600
4-year								
Nondoctoral granting	63	48	31	36	6,500	4,300	2,000	3,400
Doctoral granting	56	39	16	33	8,800	5,200	2,200	4,000
Private, for-profit								
Less-than-2-year	74	70	58	41	3,700	3,500	1,700	3,300
2-year or more	68	63	39	52	5,100	4,700	1,700	3,800
Tuition/fees								
Less than $500	20	12	11	4	1,700	2,100	1,100	2,800
$500-999	37	26	22	10	2,200	2,300	1,400	2,500
$1,000-1,999	47	36	29	20	3,200	3,100	1,700	2,800
$2,000-3,999	56	45	31	31	4,100	3,800	1,900	3,000
$4,000-7,999	68	56	39	41	5,200	4,300	1,900	3,400
$8,000 or more	64	49	22	44	9,400	5,400	2,200	3,900
Graduate/First professional students								
Total	39	19	--	--	8,500	8,600	--	--
Degree program								
Masters	34	14	--	--	6,500	6,500	--	--
Doctorate	55	17	--	--	10,800	9,300	--	--
First professional	73	63	--	--	14,500	12,000	--	--
Other graduate	25	--	--	--	--	--	--	--

Table 2. Receipt of student financial aid by postsecondary students, 1992-93 (continued)

Student characteristics	Percent receiving:				Average aid per aided student			
	Any aid	Federal aid			Any aid	Federal aid		
		Total	Grant	Loan		Total	Grant	Loan
Graduate/First professional students								
Attendance status								
Full-time, full-year	68	44	--	--	12,200	10,200	--	--
Part-time and/or part-year	29	11	--	--	5,500	6,300	--	--

-- Not published.

Source: U.S. Department of Education, National Center of Education Statistics, Student Financing of Undergraduate Education, 1992-93 (NCES 95-202) and Student Financing of Graduate and First-Professional Education, 1992-93 (NCES 96-235), based on data from the National Postsecondary Student Aid Study, 1992-93.

Federal Student Aid Policy: A History and an Assessment

Lawrence E. Gladieux

INTRODUCTION

A famous essayist whose name escapes me once apologized to his friend for not having the time to write a shorter letter. The length of this paper exceeds the 5-10 pages suggested for the Charleston conference papers. Having been asked to present pertinent policy history, I ran short of time to make it shorter. Yet perhaps an extra allowance should be made for history on this occasion. After all, we are in part marking the 30th anniversary of the Higher Education Act (HEA) of 1965.

More to the point, an interpretation of the past may be the most useful place to start for those trying to shape better government policies aimed at helping students and families pay for higher education.

To guide readers, the first seven pages or so recount the evolution of the federal role in postsecondary student aid, highlighted by critical dates over the past 50 years. Depending on their familiarity with the history, readers may wish to make quick or selective reading of this material, then focus on the balance of the paper, which describes from this observer's vantage point the broad trends, shifts, achievements and shortfalls of the government's effort during this period.

As further background for the paper and the conference, Figures 1 and 2 and Tables 1 and 2 show the growth and changes in the mix of student aid dollars, from federal as well as state and institutional sources, in recent decades. In purchasing power (constant dollars), the total amount of aid available to students has grown more than 15-fold since 1963-64, largely because of an expanding federal investment. Although institutions supplied almost half of all aid in the early 1960s, they provide less than one-fifth in the mid-1990s. The federal government now generates over $35 billion annually in student assistance, or three-fourths of the total, the bulk in the form of federally-sponsored loans to students and their parents.

A 50-YEAR RETROSPECTIVE ON FEDERAL POLICY

The democratization of college opportunities in the United States can be traced through two centuries--from the land-grant college movement and the establishment of state universities in the 19th century to The Servicement's Readjustment Act (GI Bill), establishment of community college systems, and explosion of enrollments following World War II. Major phases in the growth of higher education have extended access to new groups in society.

43

It is in the past several decades, however, that equal opportunity has become a centerpiece of public policy toward higher education. A principal expression of this goal has been the growth of need-based student assistance. Today the federal government is by far the largest sponsor of such aid, but the establishment of this federal commitment did not come easily.

1944. GI Bill was enacted by Congress to reward veterans who had served their country during wartime and to help them catch up with their peers whose lives had not been interrupted by military service. During the 1940s and 1950s, GI Bill benefits extended higher education opportunities to thousands of men and women who otherwise might never have gone to college.

But advocates of broader federal support for higher education unrelated to military service faced an uphill struggle. In fact, aid-to-education proposals of all kinds repeatedly ran aground in Congress, blocked by civil rights and church-state controversies and fear of federal control of education. Moreover, the idea of federal scholarship support, whether based on financial need or academic merit, met resistance from those who believed students should not get a free ride. Many members of Congress at that time had worked their way through college.

1958. The Soviet launch of Sputnik finally gave Congress the occasion to justify a limited form of student assistance in the name of national security. The National Defense Education Act of 1958 provided low-interest loans for college students, with debt cancellation for those who became teachers after graduation. The law also established graduate fellowships to encourage students in the sciences, mathematics, engineering, and other strategic fields. Outright scholarships or need-based grants for undergraduate study, however, were still considered beyond the pale.

1965. The Kennedy legacy, the civil rights movement, and the Johnson Administration's War on Poverty converged in the mid-1960s to break new ground. The 89th Congress presided over the broadest sweep of social legislation since the New Deal. Along with breakthroughs in civil rights came large-scale aid to education, including the HEA.

Title IV of the HEA embodied the first explicit federal commitment to equalizing college opportunities for needy students. This goal was to be advanced through need-tested grants and through student support programs such as Upward Bound (initially part of the war on poverty legislation of 1964) and Talent Search, designed to identify and foster access for college-able students who were poor. Colleges wishing to receive an allocation of funds under the new Educational Opportunity Grants program were required to make "vigorous" efforts to identify and recruit students with "exceptional financial need." Title IV of the law also included College Work-Study (another program first ushered in as part of the War on Poverty) to subsidize employment of needy students, and the Guaranteed Student Loan (GSL) program to ease the cash-flow problems of middle-income college students and their families.

The impetus for the GSL program was mounting support in Congress for a tuition tax credit for parents with children in college. Advocates of greater access for needy students worried that enactment of a tax credit and the resulting loss of federal revenue would hurt chances of funding new programs for low-income students under the HEA. The loan program appeared to be a much less costly way to help the middle class, especially since it relied on private sources of loan capital. At least initially, it was not anticipated to draw heavily from the Federal Treasury, so that federal resources could be focused primarily on the neediest students.

1968. Congress reauthorized the HEA three years later with only slight modifications. A new program, Special Services for the Disadvantaged, was added to the law; in combination with Upward Bound and Talent Search, they came to be known as the TRIO programs.

Although the ballooning costs of the Vietnam conflict constrained the growth of many domestic social programs, appropriations for student aid grew rapidly in the late 1960s. These monies eclipsed other forms of federal support for higher education, such as construction of academic facilities.

1972. The next reauthorization of the HEA rounded out the principal programs and the basic charter of today's federal student aid system.

During the debate leading up to this legislation, the higher education community urged Congress to enact formula-based, enrollment-driven federal aid to institutions. But legislators decided that funding aid to students was the more efficient and effective way to remove financial barriers for needy students and thus equalize opportunities for higher education. Congress also viewed student aid as a way to harness market forces for enhancing the quality of higher education. Students, voting with their feet, would take their federal aid to institutions that met their needs; less satisfactory institutions would wither.

Congress made a further point in the 1972 legislation by substituting the term "postsecondary education" for "higher education" and broadening the range of options available to students. The intent was to break the stereotype that education beyond high school meant full-time attendance in a four-year academic program leading to a baccalaureate degree. The 1972 HEA amendments extended greater federal recognition and support to career and vocational education, community colleges, and trade schools as well as to students in part-time programs.

Above all, proprietary schools gained full eligibility to participate in the programs under Title IV of the HEA. Over the next two decades, these schools would proliferate and prove uniquely adept at capturing federal student aid dollars.

Congress also expanded the types of assistance available to students. The Nixon Administration had proposed Basic Educational Opportunity Grants to replace three existing federal student aid programs administered through the colleges: Educational Opportunity Grants, National Defense Student Loans, and Work-Study. Congress refused to repeal the campus-based programs, but did adopt Basic Grants (now called Pell Grants), envisioning this new program as a foundation for all forms of aid and one that students would apply for directly to the federal government. Initially authorized at a maximum of $1,400, the Basic Grant was to provide a minimum level of resources to help assure access to higher education; the campus-based programs would provide supplemental aid to help assure student choice among programs and institutions.

State Student Incentive Grants were also authorized in 1972. The SSIG program provided federal matching dollars to induce states to enact or expand their own need-based student grant programs. And the 1972 law established the Student Loan Marketing Association (Sallie Mae) as a publicly chartered private corporation to increase liquidity and capital availability in the GSL program.

1976. Issues of quality control surfaced in the next HEA reauthorization debate; Congress may have had second thoughts about some of the educational options that had been legitimized in 1972. But Congress was more concerned about getting banks to lend money for postsecondary education. The 1976 amendments provided federal incentives for states to establish loan guarantee agencies.

Another significant expansion of the aid system was authorized with the addition of a few words to the statute. Students without high school degrees became eligible for federal assistance so long as they had the "ability to benefit" from postsecondary training.

1978. In an off-year of the reauthorization cycle, but under pressure for some kind of response to the perceived middle-income squeeze in financing college costs, Congress passed the Middle Income Student Assistance Act (MISAA) of 1978. As in 1965, tuition tax credit proposals had built up another head of steam in Congress. To head them off, congressional Democrats and the Carter Administration developed a counterproposal to widen eligibility for Pell Grants and open subsidized guaranteed loans to any student regardless of income or financial need.

1979. A year later Congress passed a little-noticed amendment assuring banks a favorable rate of return on guaranteed student loans by tying their subsidies directly and fully to changes in Treasury bill rates. (Previously the rate had been set by a group of government officials with a cap on how much lenders could receive.) With the economy moving into a period of double-digit inflation and interest rates, student loan volume and associated federal costs exploded. The problem of lender participation and capital shortage in the loan program became a thing of the past.

1980. The pressure to expand financial aid for the middle class continued through the HEA reauthorization of 1980. Outmaneuvering the Carter Administration as well as the congressional budget committees, the education authorizing committees further liberalized criteria governing need-tested aid, yet shielded the open-ended GSL from measures to curb eligibility, reduce subsidies, or otherwise control ballooning federal costs. The 1980 legislation also created offshoots of the GSL program providing supplemental borrowing opportunities for parents of dependent undergraduate students and for students who were financially independent of their parents.

1981. However, the legislative expansion of 1980 was short-lived. Ronald Reagan was elected president, and domestic social programs faced a budgetary onslaught in the early 1980s. Many provisions of the 1980 reauthorization were repealed in the 1981 budget reconciliation, need was reintroduced as a condition of eligibility for guaranteed loans, and an origination fee of 5 percent was imposed on borrowers as a cost-cutting measure.

The growth curve in federal student aid leveled off sharply in the first half of the 1980s. Grant support dropped, as did the overall purchasing power of student aid. Loan eligibility and subsidies were trimmed; but as an entitlement that had become popular with the middle class, guaranteed student loans proved the most resilient form of aid. Loan volume continued to grow, although at rates slower than between 1978 and 1981.

1986. In the mid-1980s, in the face of continued Reagan Administration threats to the programs, congressional advocates of student aid adopted a damage control strategy. A reauthorization that was basically status quo was the result. Legislators voiced concern about the increasing reliance of students on loans, but they came up with no effective remedies to combat this trend as tuition at both public and private institutions spiraled well ahead of inflation. Federal borrowing ceilings were increased.

1987-90. Loan volume shot up again after the 1986 HEA reauthorization. Meanwhile, media attention and public concern focused on mounting student loan defaults and proprietary trade school abuse. Through the annual budget reconciliation process, Congress forced a series of changes aimed at reducing defaults and effecting other cost savings.

1992. Leaders of the reauthorization process in Congress again said they wanted to achieve a better balance between grant and loan support for students, boosting grant aid and reducing reliance on loans. But the 1992 legislative outcome continued the policy drift in the opposite direction.

The prospect of a post-cold war peace dividend had fueled hopes that Pell Grants might be turned into an entitlement or mandated spending program with automatic annual increases for inflation. But the peace dividend never materialized, leaving no room under the budget rules for such an expansion.

After the attempt to create a Pell Grant entitlement failed, Congress followed the path of less resistance by boosting dollar ceilings for the loan programs. In addition to raising the borrowing limits for students, Congress uncapped the Parent Loan (PLUS) program, thus allowing parents to borrow up to the total cost of attendance minus any other funds the student might have received. In estimating the federal costs of all the new borrowing authority, House and Senate sponsors assumed that low market-interest rates would continue, thus minimizing the projected expense of the changes and avoiding any violation of spending caps mandated in the budget process.

The 1992 legislation also created a new, unsubsidized loan option not restricted by financial need. This was designed to make loans available to those Americans in the middle-income range who had been squeezed out of eligibility for the subsidized guaranteed loan. ("Unsubsidized" means that the government does not pay interest costs while the borrower is in school.)

This legislation further established a consolidated federal methodology for determining student and family ability to pay that applies to all Title IV programs, not just Pell Grants. The net impact of the new methodology (which many states and institutions also use as the basis for awarding their own funds) is a dramatic reduction in expected family and student contributions, extending potential eligibility for aid (particularly loans) to a substantially larger portion of the middle class.

Like the responses to the 1978 and 1986 legislation, student loan volume has once again ballooned as a result of the 1992 reauthorization. Increased loan limits, introduction of unsubsidized loans, and changes in need analysis boosted student and parent borrowing by almost $10 billion between academic years 1992-93 and 1994-95--nearly a two-thirds increase in just two years. (See Table 1.)

The 1992 legislation also authorized a demonstration program to test the feasibility and cost effectiveness of the federal government administering student loans directly through postsecondary institutions as an alternative to guaranteeing loans through private banks. Finally, Congress in 1992 sought to tighten oversight of institutions participating in federal aid programs by redefining the responsibilities of the gatekeeping triad--the Department of Education, postsecondary accreditation bodies, and the states. The principal new thrust placed more reliance on states through the creation of State Postsecondary Review Entities (SPREs) to help determine institutional eligibility under Title IV.

1993. Even as Congress hammered out the 1992 legislation, presidential candidate Bill Clinton was on the campaign trail promising a complete overhaul of the student aid system if he was elected. He repeatedly cited defaults, excessive bank fees, high government costs of the loan program, and the aid system's overall lack of effectiveness in making college affordable. Emphasizing the responsibilities of those who receive aid, Clinton called for benefits that students could earn through community service or reimburse at rates geared to their future income.

A year later, in fact, President Clinton won Congressional passage of the Student Loan Reform Act of 1993, altering the way student loans are financed, originated, serviced, and repaid. The 1993 legislation greatly expanded on the Direct Loan demonstration program authorized in 1992, calling for at least 60 percent conversion of federal student loan volume from guaranteed to direct lending over a five-year period. The act also called for more flexibility in how borrowers repay, including an income-contingent plan that calibrates monthly repayments to a percentage of the borrower's income for up to 25 years.

In his first year in office, the President also won passage of a national and community service program, though on a much smaller scale and with much less of a link to the student aid system than he had called for during the campaign. As enacted and funded, the National Service Corps provides benefits to only a tiny percentage of federal student aid recipients.

1994. Having made student aid reform a top domestic policy commitment, and having won early legislative victories to support plans in this area, the Clinton Administration struggled to fulfill another campaign promise--to streamline the regulatory process for student aid programs. Yet to implement the host of legislative initiatives passed in both 1992 and 1993-- everything from SPREs to direct lending and income-contingent repayment--the Department of Education ultimately generated more than 70 rule-making packages. The volume and complexity of the new rules as well as contention with the education community over many of them led to a sense that the regulatory process was as overwhelming as ever.

At the same time, the Clinton Administration sought to project a longer-range, Phase II agenda of student aid reform. The Department of Education held regional hearings around the country to test reactions and gather ideas on how federal aid might be further restructured, better targeted, and simplified. However, the Administration's Phase II vision sparked little enthusiasm among aid administrators coping with the broad scale of change already under way, or with college leaders preoccupied with the Administration's SPRE proposals. The Administration's Phase II designs were also overtaken by political events, namely the 1994 election.

1995. With new Republican majorities in both Houses of Congress, the policy environment in Washington is as unsettled as it has been since the early 1980s. The federal commitment to education and other domestic social programs once again hangs in the balance. The outcome of today's hectic debates in Washington is anyone's guess. The only certainty is that almost everything government does--and how it should be done--is on the table.

POLICY SHIFTS

A half century after the initial GI Bill, three decades since the establishment of federally guaranteed student loans, and more than two decades following the creation of a national basic grant program, both the central commitment to federal support for higher education and the mechanisms of such support are under attack. This is an important time to take stock of government policies, how they have evolved over time, and what they have accomplished.

What has changed since the principal federal aid programs of today were first legislated? In one sense, not a great deal. The student-based strategy Congress adopted in the 1960s and 1970s--granting and lending to students rather than institutions--has become the system's hallmark. Today more than 90 percent of U.S. Department of Education funds for postsecondary education are provided in the form of student financial aid. With additions and elaborations, in fact, the same programs are in place as were established a quarter century ago.

Underlying policies, however, have shifted. On many counts, today's aid system looks much different from what the early legislative framers envisioned.

Growing Reliance on Loans. Above all, the drift toward a system that relies primarily on student debt to finance higher tuition has turned the original commitment to equal opportunity on its head. The legislation of the 1960s and early 1970s established a commitment to help disadvantaged students through need-based grant programs, while helping middle-class families through government-guaranteed (but minimally subsidized) private bank loans.

Today, loans are far and away the largest source of aid, even for the lowest-income students. Since the mid-1970s, when student borrowing began to grow, loans have increased from about one-fifth to nearly two-fifths of all available student aid. Federal student loans provided over $26 billion in 1994-95, almost five times the size of the Pell Grant program that was meant to be the system's foundation. (See Table 1.)

The Clinton student loan reforms over the long haul could help redress the loan-grant imbalance. Part of the intent of direct lending from its conception has been lower federal costs compared with the elaborate subsidy structure of the guaranteed loan program. At the moment, the shift to direct lending--and the projected cost savings--are being challenged by the Republican Congress. To the extent that the direct lending program does survive and savings do result, more federal resources could become available for investment in Pell and other grant aid. On the other hand, direct lending could lead to more borrowing; to the extent that it succeeds in streamlining delivery of loans, it may make loan capital that much more accessible and attractive.[1]

Erosion of Need-Based Standards. Meanwhile, the antipoverty origins of the 1960s legislation have faded into history as eligibility for federal student aid has been stretched up the economic ladder. This development has been double-edged. On the one hand, broader eligibility has popularized programs with the middle class and, therefore, strengthened their political base. The stronger political foundation resulting from the middle-income legislation of 1978 probably helped to protect these programs from what could have been worse cutbacks in the early 1980s. On the other hand, the shift has diluted the federal emphasis on subsidies for low-income students and led to the predominance of loans in the mix of available aid.

---

[1] See Richard W. Moore, "Proprietary Schools and Direct Loans," Select Issues in the Federal Direct Loan Program (US Department of Education, 1994), pp. 13-24.

The changes in need analysis enacted in 1992 have produced another expansion in middle-income eligibility, inflating officially recognized need by several billion dollars. But with no corresponding increase in available funds, more "need" is chasing roughly the same number of available dollars. The probable effect is that scarce dollars have shifted up the income scale, at the expense of more disadvantaged students and families.

Growth in Self-Supporting, Non-Traditional Students. In the past several HEA reauthorizations, Congress has also sought to adjust aid policies to better meet the needs of older and part-time students. The original programs and procedures of need analysis were designed for families with dependent children who attend college full time. However, growing numbers of students are beyond the traditional age group, attend less than full time, and have ongoing family and work responsibilities while in school. Over the past two decades, the proportion of postsecondary students over age 25 has roughly doubled, from one-fifth to two-fifths of all students. Students qualifying as independent or self-supporting under federal rules now constitute a substantial majority of Title IV aid recipients.

How the government should support such students has become an ongoing policy concern in the 1990s. In 1992, Congress liberalized eligibility for some categories of independent and part-time students, but restricted it for single independent students. Policy makers remain concerned that the aid system is insufficiently sensitive to the wide-ranging circumstances of an increasingly diverse postsecondary population. At the same time, trade-offs are involved; outside of entitlement programs, expanding eligibility for independent adult students potentially reduces the dollars available to dependent students from low-income families.

Use of Aid for Short-Term Vocational Training. When Congress decided to "broaden the mainstream" of postsecondary education in the early 1970s, no one had envisioned the burgeoning of the proprietary trade school industry. The proprietary sector has been highly responsive to federal student aid policies.[2] It flourished in response to the postwar GI Bill, and once fully eligible for programs under Title IV of the Higher Education Act, the industry again expanded rapidly in the late 1970s and 1980s. Entrepreneurs created hundreds of new for-profit schools and programs during this period, all enrolling aid-eligible students, many of them focusing on low-income inner-city areas. Alongside training traditionally offered by the proprietary sector in secretarial work and business, refrigeration, welding, auto mechanics, and the like, new programs sprouted offering training for truck drivers, security guards, retail clerks, and nannies.

By the late 1980s proprietary school students received one-fourth of all Pell Grant funds and more than one-third of guaranteed loan volume. Program abuse and disproportionately high loan default rates in the trade school sector, however, attracted mounting publicity, prompting a series of legislative and regulatory remedies. The proprietary school industry and its share of federal student aid funds have since contracted significantly. Proprietary schools

---

[2] Ibid.

nonetheless continue to have a major stake in federal aid. Of roughly 7,500 institutions now eligible for the Title IV programs, about 4,000 are proprietary. Students at these institutions currently receive one-sixth of Pell Grants and one-tenth of all guaranteed loans.

Compared to 25 years ago, when perhaps 2,000 collegiate institutions participated in federal student aid programs, today's regulatory dilemma for the Department of Education is the sheer number and diversity of schools and the kinds of education and training supported by Title IV. A focus on short-term vocational training fits with the national agenda of retraining and upgrading the skills of the work force. But student aid is not necessarily the most effective mechanism for financing such training. There is also virtually no coordination of Title IV aid with the substantial amount of support for postsecondary employment training provided by other federal programs and agencies.[3]

Use of Aid for Remediation. Over time, more and more federal student aid dollars have been provided to students who are not prepared to do college-level work. This trend toward funding remediation has occurred for two reasons. First is the "ability to benefit" provision added to the law in 1976, which allowed hundreds of thousands of non-high school graduates to qualify for Title IV aid. The standards used to determine which students can benefit have been low and largely unregulated. For a long time, the tests were developed and administered by the schools to which the students were applying. More recently, a variety of federally-sanctioned independent tests have been in use. However, the "passing grade" has been low enough to allow all but a handful of students to qualify for aid on this basis.

The second reason for the trend toward Title IV funding of remediation is simply the inadequate preparation of large numbers of high school graduates. The ongoing debate over K-12 school reform and standards underscores the fact that too many high school graduates cannot yet do college-level work. In recognition of this underpreparedness, the existing federal student aid legislation allows students taking remedial courses to receive federal aid for up to one year of course work. But the regulations governing this limitation are unclear as to how eligibility is to be terminated, and many students taking remedial work continue to receive aid for periods longer than one year.

ACHIEVEMENTS AND SHORTFALLS

The above historical review suggests that the objectives, mechanisms, and constituencies of federal student aid today are considerably more diffuse and complex than they were a quarter century ago. Thus gauging the impact and success of aid policies over this period is far from cut-and-dried, and this paper will only scratch the surface of such an evaluation.

---

[3] See Janet S. Hansen, Editor, Preparing for the Workplace: Charting a Course for Federal Postsecondary Training Policy, National Academy Press, 1994.

Federal student aid has clearly been an important force in shaping American postsecondary education since World War II. Although causes and effects are arguable, federal aid has no doubt helped fuel a half century of explosive growth in college attendance by Americans, and it surely has had something to do with producing the diversity of today's student population.

Yet one casualty of time has been naive expectations about what could be accomplished through student aid to advance national goals of educational equity, quality, and affordability. The balance of this paper discusses these goals and presents indicators relating to the effectiveness of student aid in fostering them.[4]

Access. Above all, the problem of unequal opportunity has proved more intractable than anyone anticipated in the early years of the Higher Education Act. In the late 1960s and early 1970s, widely-cited reports from the Bureau of the Census showed that a college-age youth from a family with an income over $15,000 was nearly five times more likely to be enrolled in higher education than one from a family with an income of less than $3,000.[5] The new student aid programs were to be on the cutting edge of policy to close such gaps.

Today college-age young people from the highest-income range by Census categories ($75,000 or more) are three and a half times more likely to be enrolled in college as those from the lowest income range (under $15,000).[6] Although shifts in the distribution of income probably invalidate a precise comparison of Census data over the intervening decades, these figures may suggest a measure of improvement in access to college opportunities during this period. But the more certain point is that large gaps stubbornly persist.

Many other statistics underscore the continued socioeconomic disparities in access to and successful completion of higher education programs. Among recent high school graduates, those from low-income families are still half as likely to enroll in college by the fall following their graduation as those from high-income families. The enrollment rate of recent black high school graduates (47 percent in 1991) still lags behind that of whites (64 percent); the rate in 1991 for Hispanic high school graduates was 53 percent.[7] In 1993, whites 25 to 29 years of

---

[4] For a more extensive discussion of indicators relating to the effectiveness of student aid, see Lawrence E. Gladieux and Arthur M. Hauptman, The College Aid Quandary: Access, Quality, and the Federal Role, The Brookings Institution and The College Board, forthcoming 1995.

[5] For example, see Toward Equal Opportunity for Higher Education, Report of the Panel on Financing Low Income and Minority Students in Higher Education, College Entrance Examination Board, New York, 1973, p. 11.

[6] U.S. Department of Commerce, Bureau of the Census, School Enrollment--Social and Economic Characteristics of Students: October 1993, Current Population Reports P20-479, Table 16 "Families by Full-Time College Enrollment of Dependent Members 18 to 24 Years Old, by Family Income, Race, and Hispanic Origin: October 1993."

[7] U.S. Department of Education, National Center for Education Statistics, The Condition of Education 1994, p.40.

age were still twice as likely to have completed four years of college as blacks, and three times more likely than Hispanics.[8]

Such gaps in opportunity, and the failure of student aid policies to close them, should probably not come as a surprise. For one thing, federal student aid in its conception was primarily about helping those who otherwise might not have access to higher education; in their evolution, federal policies have become as much (or more) about relieving the economic burden for those who would probably pursue postsecondary programs without such aid. Moreover, it is clear that state tuition, subsidy, and funding policies are at least as important in determining patterns of enrollment and access as what the federal government can achieve through its investment in student aid.

We also know more today about the complexity of the college-going process. Enrollment and success in higher education are functions of many factors--academic aptitude and prior schooling, family and community attitudes, motivation, and awareness of opportunities--not just ability to pay. Above all, there appear to be huge and growing disparities in the capacity of K-12 educational systems to prepare young people for the world beyond high school. Higher education, much less student aid as a financing strategy, cannot alone redress social deficits and imbalances that appear to threaten our country's future.

Access to What? The notion that having students vote with their feet would somehow assure quality in the postsecondary education marketplace was a dubious proposition from the start. More than a quarter century later, it is clear that the marketplace rationale begged important questions of institutional quality and accountability, as well as consumer information, awareness, and protection.

Federal student aid programs have been plagued by institutions that defraud both taxpayers and students, offering programs of little or no educational or vocational value, or that are so poorly managed they do not serve students effectively. High student loan default rates, as well as low completion and placement rates for students who receive aid, have reflected these problems and galvanized public concern.

Much of the trouble has come in the for-profit sector; but the baggage of fraud and abuse has encumbered the entire student aid effort and triggered tighter rules affecting all of postsecondary education. In part, this reflects successful lobbying by the proprietary school industry, which has blocked proposals to remove trade schools from participanting in Title IV programs or authorize separate regulatory controls over them. It also suggests that policy makers are not necessarily persuaded that all problems relating to consumer protection and lax educational standards are in the non-collegiate sector. Policy makers are increasingly prone to examine more critically the effectiveness and performance of traditional higher education.

---

[8] U.S. Department of Commerce, Bureau of the Census, Educational Attainment in The United States: March 1993 and 1992, Current Population Reports P20-476, Table 18 "Percent of Persons 25 years Old and Over Who Have Completed High School or College, by Race, Hispanic Origin and Sex: Selected Years 1940 to 1993."

From the beginning, federal student aid policy has been shaped by a commitment to access. The legacy of access to higher education is deeply ingrained in our public values. Debates over student aid policy have typically centered on whether policy changes would hinder or expand access for disadvantaged students. But we have learned that access does not assure quality; in fact, access can ill-serve students if they do not complete their education or graduate without the skills they need to succeed.

Low-income, at-risk students are actually the most ill-served when student aid incentives encourage their enrollment in programs subject to minimal quality control. In such programs they have, at best, only modest chances of success; at worst, they are left with no job, a defaulted loan, and a bad credit record.

Affordability. In the 1970s, family income levels increased faster than tuition; growth in student aid outstripped both tuition increases and growth in the number of eligible students; and grant aid was more common than borrowing.

All these trend lines, however, turned against college affordability in the 1980s and 1990s. Family income has generally remained flat and has been far outpaced by tuition increases, which at both public and private four-year institutions have averaged at least twice the rate of inflation since 1980. Tuitions have risen annually by more than 8 percent over this period, while annual growth in the Consumer Price Index has averaged about 4 percent. Public sector prices have increased most sharply in the 1990s, rising at 3 times the rate of inflation as the economy and revenues in most states have declined.

Student aid, meanwhile, has failed to close the gap between family income and college prices. The real value of total aid available to students has increased since 1980. However, the growth has been primarily in the form of loans and has not kept pace with growth in tuition levels or in the eligible student population.

In the mid-1990s, tuition increases have moderated slightly. According to the College Board's annual survey of colleges, tuition in both public and private four-year higher education institutions has risen 6 percent in each of the past two years, still twice the Consumer Price Index but less than the rate of tuition growth in the early 1990s. More and more private institutions worry about pricing themselves out of the market and are trying to restructure their operations to contain costs. In the public sector, economic recovery may have relieved some of the pressure on tuition as a revenue source in state budgets. But the tuition spiral is not likely to end, nor is student aid likely to catch up, any time soon.

To say that federal aid programs have fallen short of expectations for achieving broad national goals is surely not to pronounce the effort an abject failure or to encourage those who would decimate the federal commitment in this area. It is, rather, to say that we sorely need constructive debate and proposals to strengthen the system that we have.

The foregoing review of history sets the stage for asking questions essential to any attempt to envision better aid policies in the future. We need to revisit first principles. Does the case for federal investment in higher education remain as valid today as it was in the 1960s and 1970s? Are the goals discussed in this paper--access, quality, affordability--the right ones? If so, how should we define and operationalize them? Can we stem the policy drift toward a system that places more and more of the cost burden on students and their families? Should we? For all students? Some students? Which students? Do we need to strike a better balance between the values of equity and quality? If so, how? Do we have the right set of programs in place to get the job done? How can we reduce the system's complexity from the point of view of students, parents, and administrators?

These questions are just for starters. Other commissioned papers will provoke discussion in Charleston by presenting not only questions but blueprints for the future. To the extent that such discussion ultimately helps to sharpen policy and make the system more coherent and effective, the federal aid programs will be in a stronger position to compete for scarce resources, contribute to the country's economic future, and sustain the American promise of opportunity into the 21st century.

Lawrence E. Gladieux is executive director for policy analysis of the College Board, a national association of schools and colleges that provides testing, financial aid, guidance, training, and other services to the education community. He has built the reputation of the Board's Washington, DC, office for reliable analysis of trends and issues in higher education finance, student aid, education reform, and college admissions. He is editor of Radical Reform or Incremental Change? Student Loan Policy Alternatives for the 1990s (The College Board, 1989) and co-author of Congress and the Colleges: The National Politics of Higher Education (Lexington Books, 1976).

Figure 1

Amount of Aid to Postsecondary Students
1963-64 to 1993-94

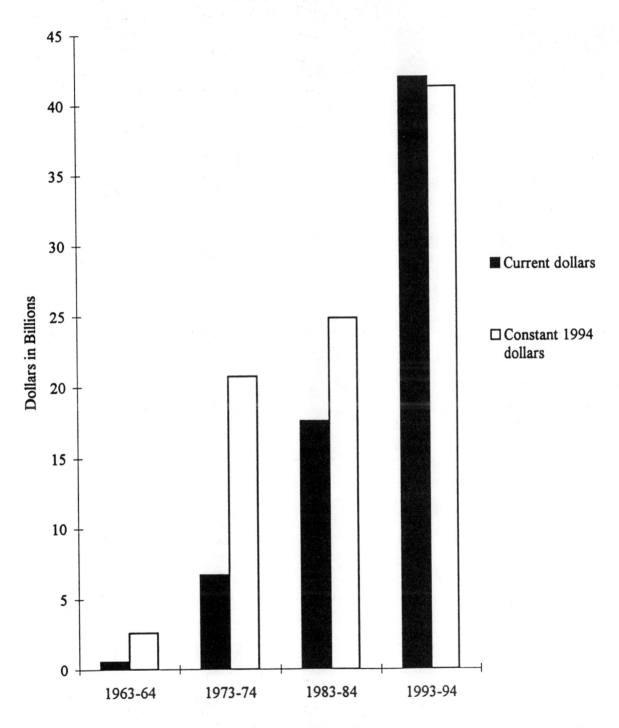

Source: The College Board, *Trends in Student Aid: 1985 to 1995.*

Figure 2

Composition of Aid to Postsecondary Students
1963-64 to 1993-94

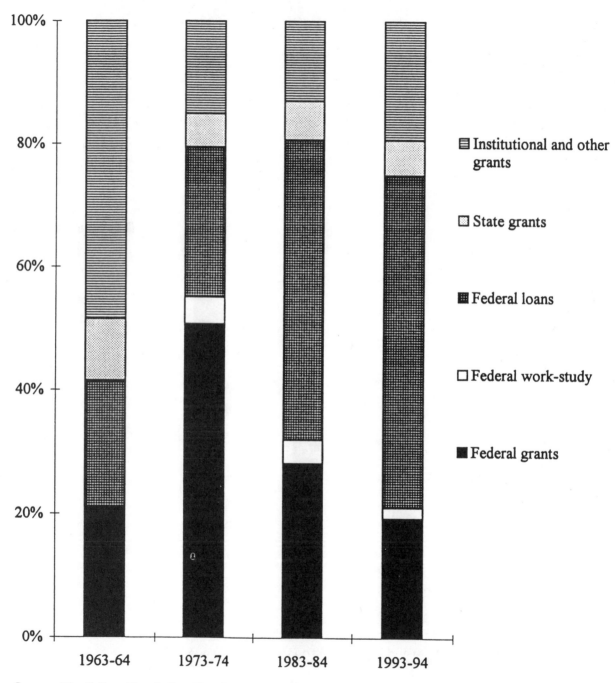

Source: The College Board, *Trends in Student Aid: 1985 to 1995.*

Table 1. Aid Awarded to Postsecondary Students in Current Dollars
(in Millions)

Academic Year

Generally Supported Programs	1985-86	1986-87	1987-88	1988-89	1989-90	1990-91	1991-92	1992-93	Estimated 1993-94	Preliminary 1994-95
Generally Available Aid										
Pell Grants	3,567	3,441	3,736	4,471	4,768	4,910	5,777	6,177	5,652	5,650
SEOG	410	400	419	422	445	453	498	554	564	554
SSIG	76	73	75	72	71	59	62	71	72	73
CWS	656	629	635	625	663	728	760	780	771	760
Perkins Loans	703	763	805	874	903	870	868	892	919	972
Income Contingent Loans	0	0	5	5	6	6	5	5	0	0
Ford Direct Student Loans	0	0	0	0	0	0	0	0	0	1,737
(Subsidized Stafford Loans)	0	0	0	0	0	0	0	0	0	(1,089)
(Unsubsidized Stafford Loans)	0	0	0	0	0	0	0	0	0	(478)
(PLUS)	0	0	0	0	0	0	0	0	0	(170)
Family Education Loans	8,839	9,102	11,385	11,985	12,151	12,669	13,993	14,914	21,182	22,936
(Subsidized Stafford Loans)	(8,328)	(8,330)	(9,119)	(9,319)	(9,508)	(10,002)	(10,805)	(10,937)	(14,123)	(14,104)
(Unsubsidized Stafford Loans)	0	0	0	0	0	0	0	(323)	(2,033)	(7,139)
(SLS)	(269)	(520)	(1,830)	(2,015)	(1,835)	(1,710)	(2,022)	(2,375)	(3,477)	(32)
(PLUS)	(242)	(252)	(436)	(651)	(808)	(957)	(1,165)	(1,279)	(1,550)	(1,660)
Subtotal	14,251	14,408	17,060	18,455	19,007	19,694	21,963	23,392	29,161	32,681
Specially Directed Aid										
Veterans	864	783	762	724	790	679	876	1,037	1,192	1,410
Military	342	361	349	341	364	369	394	393	405	421
Other Grants	67	74	92	102	110	118	160	162	168	186
Other Loans	372	316	298	332	355	345	367	411	456	405
Subtotal	1,646	1,534	1,502	1,498	1,620	1,510	1,796	2,003	2,221	2,423
Total Federal Aid	15,897	15,942	18,562	19,952	20,627	21,204	23,759	25,395	31,382	35,104
State Grant Programs	1,311	1,432	1,503	1,581	1,719	1,860	1,968	2,125	2,375	2,665
Institutional and Other Grants	2,962	3,371	3,808	3,978	4,951	5,761	6,679	7,485	8,233	9,057
Total Federal, State, and Institutional Aid	20,169	20,745	23,873	25,511	27,297	28,825	32,406	35,006	41,990	46,826

Details may not add to totals due to rounding.

Source: Trends in Student Aid: 1985 to 1995, The College Board

Table 2. Aid Awarded to Postsecondary Students in Constant 1994 Dollars
(in Millions)

Academic Year

Federally Supported Programs	1985-86	1986-87	1987-88	1988-89	1989-90	1990-91	1991-92	1992-93	Estimated 1993-94	Prelimir 199
Generally Available Aid										
Pell Grants	4,866	4,590	4,786	5,477	5,570	5,436	6,199	6,427	5,731	5
SEOG	559	533	537	518	520	501	535	576	572	
SSIG	103	97	97	89	83	65	67	74	73	
CWS	895	839	814	766	775	806	815	812	782	
Perkins Loans	959	1,018	1,031	1,070	1,054	964	931	928	932	
Income Contingent Loans	0	0	6	6	6	6	5	5	0	
Ford Direct Student Loans	0	0	0	0	0	0	0	0	0	1
(Subsidized Stafford Loans)	0	0	0	0	0	0	0	0	0	(1,
(Unsubsidized Stafford Loan	0	0	0	0	0	0	0	0	0	(
(PLUS)	0	0	0	0	0	0	0	0	0	(
Family Education Loans	12,056	12,141	14,584	14,681	14,196	14,028	15,015	15,518	21,480	22
(Subsidized Stafford Loans)	(11,360)	(11,112)	(11,681)	(11,415)	(11,108)	(11,075)	(11,594)	(11,381)	(14,321)	(13,
(Unsubsidized Stafford Loan	0	0	0	0	0	0	0	(336)	(2,061)	(7,
(SLS)	(367)	(694)	(2,344)	(2,468)	(2,143)	(1,894)	(2,170)	(2,471)	(3,526)	
(PLUS)	(330)	(336)	(559)	(797)	(944)	(1,059)	(1,250)	(1,331)	(1,572)	(1,
Subtotal	19,439	19,219	21,854	22,606	22,206	21,806	23,567	24,340	29,571	32
Specially Directed Aid										
Veterans	1,178	1,045	976	887	923	752	940	1,079	1,209	1
Military	467	481	447	417	426	408	422	409	411	
Other Grants	92	98	118	125	128	130	171	169	170	
Other Loans	508	422	382	407	415	382	394	428	462	
Subtotal	2,245	2,046	1,924	1,835	1,892	1,672	1,927	2,085	2,252	2,
Total Federal Aid	21,684	21,265	23,778	24,441	24,098	23,479	25,494	26,425	31,823	34,
State Grant Programs	1,788	1,911	1,926	1,936	2,008	2,059	2,112	2,212	2,408	2,
Institutional and Other Grants	4,040	4,496	4,878	4,873	5,784	6,379	7,166	7,788	8,349	8,
Total Federal, State, and Institutional Aid	27,511	27,672	30,581	31,250	31,890	31,917	34,772	36,425	42,580	46,

Details may not add to totals due to rounding.

Source: Trends in Student Aid: 1985 to 1995, The College Board

Cut the Cloth to Fit the Student:
Tailoring the Federal Role in Postsecondary Education and Training

Arthur M. Hauptman

Introduction

Amendments in 1972 to the Higher Education Act (HEA) of 1965 established student aid in the form of grants, loans and work-study as the federal policy vehicle of choice for expanding opportunities in postsecondary education and training in this country. Decisions since 1972 have reinforced the hegemony of student aid and underscored the federal belief in putting money in the pockets of students and having them vote with their feet.

Within this student aid framework, there has been pressure over time to expand eligibility to include more and more students in the federal aid programs. As in every generalization, this one has its exceptions: eligibility for loan subsidies was capped in 1981 to stem a massive expansion of borrowing, and the eligibility for aid of financially independent single students was sharply restricted in 1992. By and large, however, federal student aid policies have been more inclusive than exclusive.

The federal government also has tended to treat all students and institutions alike. Its policies typically have sought to make as many students as possible eligible for all forms of aid. Similarly, one set of federal rules and regulations has applied to all participating institutions. Again, there are exceptions to the rule: graduate and professional school students are not eligible for need-based grant programs; loan programs have been created to aid specific groups of students and to help parents; and those institutions that perform badly are targeted for elimination from the federal programs. But overall, there has been a strong federal culture to have uniform rules for all students and institutions.

To meet the very demanding national objectives of increasing access, keeping college affordable, raising retention and completion rates, and improving quality, I argue in this paper that there should be greater differentiation in federal policies toward both students and institutions. Federal aid programs should be tailored to meet the wide-ranging needs of different groups of students. Federal rules and regulations also should vary in how they treat different categories of institutions.

In this paper, I further argue that federal policies should move beyond student aid to include institutional incentives and tax provisions. Such a mix of policies may prove more effective in meeting certain goals, such as increasing retention or improving quality rather than having the federal government continue to rely solely on student aid to achieve all its objectives.

The first section of the paper discusses why existing federal policies may not have achieved their objectives. The second section suggests a strategy for the future that might prove more effective in promoting access, choice, retention and quality.

ASSESSING THE EFFECTIVENESS OF THE FEDERAL STUDENT AID PROGRAMS

Much has been written and said about the decision in 1972 to shift federal policy to a strategy focused on student aid. But the Education Amendments of 1972 and subsequent funding decisions actually consisted of two related but not identical strategies: one was the decision to rely on student aid rather than have the government provide general support to institutions. The second was to provide most student aid directly to students rather than through the campus-based aid programs that already existed.

A number of implicit policies have evolved over time from these two explicit decisions in 1972. Two important ones are:

- First, that one size tends to fit all when it comes to student aid -- all postsecondary students to the extent feasible should be eligible for the same set of aid programs, and

- Second, that loans would be used to fill whatever gaps might arise from the shortfalls in funding and the growth in need. As a result, loans have come to dominate the student aid landscape in ways that few policy makers in 1972 could have imagined.

How Well Have the Federal Programs Worked Since Enactment of the HEA in 1965 and Adoption of a Student-Aid-Based Strategy in 1972?

On the positive side, federal aid has helped millions of students go to college who otherwise would have been unable to attend. Federal aid, particularly loans, has greatly expanded the range of choices that students have in where they go to college. The numbers of low-income and minority college students have increased dramatically over the past three decades, at rates much faster than the growth of these groups in the population.

But a number of other indices suggest the federal programs are not working as well as they could or should. Unacceptably high default rates are only the most obvious sign of trouble. Equally troublesome, if not as visible, has been the inability over the past three decades to close the gap in college participation and retention rates between students from low- and high-income families and between white, black, and Hispanic students.

One way to assess the effectiveness of the federal aid programs is to compare performance to the various policy goals espoused in the legislation and its amendments. These goals include: increasing access, keeping college affordable (providing greater choice), raising retention, and improving quality.

Increasing Access. While much concern has been expressed about the need for more access to American postsecondary education, it arguably remains the most accessible system in the world. More than 5 percent of all Americans attend some form of postsecondary education every year; that is astounding by international standards. Student aid, particularly grants, has undoubtedly played a major role in providing this access. But many other factors, particularly the willingness of states to invest in public institutions thereby keeping their tuitions low, also have been key components in providing greater access.

Keeping College Affordable. Although a spate of reports decry the growing unaffordability of college, high participation rates suggest that American higher education is still affordable. ("Affordability" seems to have replaced the term "choice" that was popular in earlier policy discussions.) The perception of unaffordability or lack of choice stems mostly from the high tuitions charged by private institutions. But the growing availability of student loans in the face of rising tuitions is one of the most important factors in the stabilization of private college enrollments as a share of all college enrollments over the past two decades. This stability is in sharp contrast to the preceding quarter century when the private college share of all students fell from one-half to one-quarter.

Raising Retention. Two of the less discussed but more troubling trends over the past quarter century have been the decline in the proportion of students who complete their degree and the time it takes to attain a degree. Less than one-quarter of students who now enter a four-year program complete it; completion rates for community college students are much lower. Moreover, the average time-to-degree, especially in public institutions, has lengthened over time. Although there are many reasons for these disturbing trends, there is little evidence to suggest that student aid has been an effective tool in raising retention or completion rates.

Improving Quality. Much rhetoric has been devoted to the notion that the quality of all education and training in America, including postsecondary, must be improved in order for us to remain competitive in the global marketplace. But the federal student aid programs from their inception have placed a much higher priority on providing access than on ensuring quality. Student aid programs contain minimal standards of performance. This lack of attention to quality can be seen in the federal government's willingness to provide financial aid, especially loans, to students who have not demonstrated an ability to do college-level work. The great difficulty in removing clearly abusive institutions from eligibility to participate in the federal aid programs is another indicator of the inattention to quality concerns. It is fair to say that of the four policy objectives listed here, the student aid programs have been least effective in promoting the goal of better quality.

Why Haven't the Federal Aid Programs Been More Effective?

Many argue that inadequate funding is the reason federal student aid has not worked better. But that surely is not the only answer. Perhaps a better question is: With the funding that has been available, why haven't the federal programs achieved more?

One explanation is that the premises underlying the federal aid programs have not been fulfilled. For example, a strategy that relies on consumer choice must provide adequate and accurate information to consumers. Too often, this has not been the case.

Relying on aid recipients to vote with their feet requires the government to ensure that students receive a quality education at the institution they choose. This premise, too, often has been unfulfilled as evidenced by the many questionable institutions that qualify to receive federal student aid funds.

Another premise of the student aid strategy was that the availability of aid itself should not influence the price that institutions charge. But there is reasonable evidence that a number of trade schools have set their tuitions based on federal aid availability. (And with recent increases in loan limits, there is reason to be concerned that this problem could spread to nonprofit colleges and universities in the future.)

The federal government's tendency both to expand eligibility and to be uniform in its treatment of students and institutions also may have restricted the effectiveness of the student aid programs. Efforts to expand eligibility, no matter how well intentioned, have meant that less is available for the initially intended beneficiaries. Treating students uniformly has limited the capability of the federal programs to meet the much different needs of various groups of students. Oddly, this federal tendency toward uniformity runs counter to the great diversity in higher education that we readily acknowledge and favor.

The "failure" of federal student aid may also be a case of unrealistic expectations. Since 1972, policy makers have come to believe that the problems higher education faces -- accumulated over decades through policy decisions at federal, state, and institutional levels -- can be solved through a set of federal aid programs that represent 10 percent or less of all resources devoted to the postsecondary enterprise. This is simply too great a burden on any one set of policies, no matter how well-funded or well-devised they may be. (And most observers agree, federal student aid has been neither well-funded nor well-designed.)

Given the tremendous diversity of the 20 million or so students who attend postsecondary education and training each year, it is unrealistic to expect that the same set of policies will be best for all of them. In this context, it is not surprising that older and part-time students do not benefit as much from an aid system designed largely for full-time students.

Federal student aid may also have been ineffective because it ignores or fails to leverage the states, the largest governmental investor in higher education. Federal policies typically take as a starting point the existing pattern of state support of institutions, public sector tuitions, and state student aid. The one exception to this rule is the State Student Incentive Grant (SSIG) program that is too small to affect state behavior very much and is in perpetual danger of losing what funding it has. To the extent that state tuition and aid policies often do not mesh well with federal policy goals, more pressure is placed on the federal aid programs to achieve national policy objectives.

A STRATEGY FOR INCREASING THE RETURN ON THE FEDERAL INVESTMENT

The preceding discussion of why federal policies may not have met their stated objectives leads me to conclude the following:

First, to increase the return on the federal investment in postsecondary education and training in the future, the student aid programs should be targeted where they work best. Grants should focus on improving access for students who otherwise would be unable to attend. The principal aim of loans should be to make college more affordable for students who can most benefit from borrowing.

Second, alternatives to student aid such as institution-based approaches or tax provisions should be utilized to help those groups of students for whom the traditional aid programs have not worked well or to help achieve those objectives such as more retention and better quality where the aid programs appear to have been less effective.

Third, the federal government should be more proactive with the states by providing incentives that ensure federal and state policies work in tandem rather than at cross purposes.

To achieve these three notions, this paper suggests a new federal strategy in which the student aid programs are combined in various ways with institution-based approaches and tax provisions to meet the specific needs of the following four categories of postsecondary students:

- the growing numbers of students who require at least some remediation in order to achieve basic skills competencies;

- participants in short-term vocational training programs lasting less than one year;

- undergraduates in two- and four-year institutions and students in vocational programs lasting at least one year; and

- postbaccalaureate students enrolled in doctoral, master's and professional school programs.

In addition, federal policies should acknowledge the needs of the growing numbers of nontraditional students enrolled in any of these four levels of instruction, including less than half-time students, adult learners, and full-time workers. The remarkable growth in the numbers of nontraditional college students has been well documented. There are more older students than ever before. Many more students are also taking less than a half-time course load. More than a million students enrolled in college also work full time. The traditional college student -- enrolled full time, 18 to 22 years old, living in a dorm on campus -- is now in a distinct minority.

The sustained growth in the number of nontraditional students has occurred despite the fact that the federal aid programs are not designed with these students in mind. In the past, the traditional aid programs have been stretched to include this group of students. Instead, federal policies are needed that better meet the needs of this group of students directly.

A summary of what these strategies might entail for each group of students is shown in the matrix on the following page.

Strengthening the Student Aid Programs

The student aid component of the strategy obviously would include need-based grants, work-study, and loans. This component could be supplemented and enhanced by the use of both merit-based aid and national service provisions in selected instances. Establishing an overall annual limit on how much students can receive in federal aid also could make the aid programs more effective.

Need-Based Grants. The best weapons in the federal arsenal for providing access to a broad range of postsecondary education are need-based grants. Within feasible budgetary constraints, however, need-based grants are less likely to be effective in promoting affordability and improving retention. Need-based grants appear to be virtually ineffective if not counterproductive in improving quality. In light of this (overly broad) generalization about need-based grants, they should be used primarily to promote access. To do this, need-based grants might be divided into two components: one to support living expenses of students, and the other to help narrow the tuition differential among institutions.

Pell Grants should be available to defray the living expenses of all needy postsecondary students enrolled at least half-time in remedial programs, short-term training, and at the undergraduate level. This grant should equal a standard amount that meets basic living expenses whether a student lives on campus, off campus, or at home, minus any expected family contribution. Institutions would be responsible under this system for providing assistance to cover whatever amount of additional living expenses was entailed above this basic level.

The tuition differential component of need-based grants should be limited to undergraduates and to students in long-term vocational programs. For Pell Grants, this could be accomplished by adding a tuition differential component to the award formula, as was contemplated but ultimately rejected in the 1992 reauthorization of the HEA. Tuition differentials also should be recognized in any campus-based undergraduate grant formulas.

A MATRIX OF FEDERAL ASSISTANCE STRATEGIES

	Type of Student				
Type of Assistance	Remediation	Short-term Vocational	Undergraduate & Longer Term Vocational	Post-baccalaureate	Non-traditional
STUDENT AID PROGRAMS					
Need-Based Grants	For living expenses only	For living expenses only	For tuition, fees & living expenses	Not eligible for grants	For tuition and fees only
Merit Aid	Not eligible	Not eligible	Merit-based Pell component	Fellowships & Scholarships	Yes, where applicable
Loans	No borrowing	No borrowing	Line of credit for tuition and fees only	Line of credit for tuition & other expenses	Line of credit for tuition & other expenses
Work-Study	Not eligible	Not eligible	Yes	Yes	Not eligible
National Service	Not Applicable	Not Applicable	Loan forgiveness	Loan forgiveness	Loan forgiveness
Student Aid Packaging	Not Applicable	Not Applicable	Overall Aid Maximum	Not Applicable	Aid maximum if applicable
INSTITUTION-BASED EFFORTS					
Student Support Services	TRIO programs	Not Applicable	TRIO programs	No	No
Payments to Providers	Performance-based contracts	Performance-based contracts	Payments for Pell Grant graduates	No	Payments for Pell Grants graduates
TAX PROVISIONS					
Tax Credit/ Deduction	No, if no tuition is charged	No, if no tuition is charged	Tuition tax credit for parents; no parent loans	Tuition component of EITC	Tuition component of EITC

Merit-Based Grant Programs. Although merit-based grant programs tend not to help much in increasing access, they can be very effective in promoting better quality. They also can help in promoting choice and in improving retention to the extent that receipt of merit-aid is tied to successful completion of study at a relatively high level of achievement. Merit-aid, almost by definition, seems much more suitable for academic programs than vocational ones. As a result, merit-aid should be focused on graduate students in the form of fellowships and assistantships and, in a more limited way, on undergraduates, in both cases preferably in combination with some consideration of financial need.

Loans. The primary instrument of federal postsecondary policy and the most effective form of aid for providing greater affordability and choice are loans. But loans also have become the principal instrument for access, which is regrettable since they are far less suited for this role. In terms of retention, there are mixed views on the effectiveness of loans relative to grants. A recent GAO study concluded that grants were more effective than loans in encouraging retention. But this study compared a dollar of grant to a dollar of loan and the measure of retention was whether students completed one year of school, not whether they finished their program on time and received a degree. A more appropriate study would compare grants to the subsidy value of the loan and would use degree completion as the measure of retention, not a year of study. Such a study might well show that loans are better than grants in improving retention, because borrowers have a greater incentive to finish their programs more quickly, but loans are probably no better or worse than grants in promoting higher quality.

Loans remain the best mechanism to help undergraduates and graduate students finance their investment in themselves. Going to college on average continues to pay high dividends in the form of increased earnings, and borrowing is a perfectly reasonable way to finance this investment.

To make this correlation between loans and investment more evident, I would limit the amount of loans that undergraduates could borrow to the tuition and fees they pay, and use grants and family resources to meet their basic living costs. To the extent that post-baccalaureate students often do not pay tuition, and because we as a society do not expect parents to provide financial support to their children once they have graduated from college, graduate and professional school students should be able to borrow to pay for their non-tuition-related expenses.

To discourage institutions from raising their tuitions to increase the eligibility of their students for loans, I would limit the amount of tuition and fees that could be used in calculating eligibility for loan subsidies by subtracting expected family contributions from these federal limits. The remaining tuition and fees could be financed through institutional aid, grants, or family resources, at least for undergraduates.

For the growing numbers of students who require some form of remediation when they reach the postsecondary level, however, there has been far too much dependence in the past on loans. Every year now, at least several billion dollars are borrowed by individuals who have not demonstrated an ability to perform at the postsecondary level. Not surprisingly, these borrowers have unacceptably high rates of default. This large and growing use of loans for remediation, I believe, is the most objectionable aspect of present federal postsecondary policies.

We also have come to rely too much on loans for students in short-term vocational programs lasting one year or less. These individuals, like those in remedial academic programs, simply do not have the prospects for success that merit borrowing on the scale that now exists. By having them borrow as much as they now do, many, if not most, of these people are being further imprisoned in a world they are trying to escape.

To address this problem of excessive borrowing, students who have not demonstrated an ability to do college-level work and students in vocational programs lasting less than one year should not be allowed to borrow. Past proposals in this direction typically suggest replacing loans with grants. But this student-aid-based tradeoff is doomed to fail in the current and foreseeable budgetary environment: not enough grants can be provided to offset the loss of loans. Nor is there enough evidence that an infusion of grant money will solve the problem. I suggest that loans for these students be replaced with performance-based contracts that reward those providers of short-term training that do the best job at the lowest cost, as is discussed in the next section on institution-based approaches.

For loans to be more effective in the future, it is also important that the current crazy-quilt system be rationalized and depoliticized. The current arrangement of a dozen federal loan programs -- direct and guaranteed, subsidized and unsubsidized, student and parent -- needs a major overhaul. This discussion would entail another whole paper. Suffice it to say here that the federal student loan system of the future should: capture the best aspects of the public and private sectors; target subsidies on those borrowers who need them most at the time they need them; and provide repayment options that suit the needs of different borrowers. I also believe federal loans should be available in the form of a line of credit where students might borrow on a number of occasions over their lifetime, as long as they had satisfactorily repaid their previous student loans.

College Work-Study. The forgotten sibling of the federal student aid family is the College Work-Study program. This overshadowing is ironic in that work-study often seems to be the most popular aid program among many members of Congress who hark back to the time when they worked their way through college. (Although with the more youthful demographics of Congress, more members seem to have borrowed than worked during college.) Congressional funding levels of work-study, however, have not matched the rhetoric.

If anything, college work-study should become a more prominent part of the federal strategy because it not only helps to provide both access and affordability, it may contribute to greater retention as well. (At least one study indicates that students on work-study are more likely to complete a year's study than students who do not work.) A good argument can be made that work-study is best focused on students who are in good academic standing and, therefore, should probably not be available for students in remedial or vocational programs.

It may also be worthwhile for policy makers to consider establishing an explicit tradeoff between work-study and loans, one in which students could choose to borrow to meet their costs, and thereby free up more time for study, or work in order to minimize their debts once they graduate.

National Service. After several decades of playing a minor to nonexistent role in federal policy, National Service took center stage in the legislative debates of 1993. The issue of national service has now become so politicized, however, that it is difficult to have a rational discussion about either its merits or its flaws.

But in one aspect of national service, there may be a greater degree of bipartisanship and consensus: allowing student borrowers to repay their loans through designated forms of national and community service. (Income contingent repayment schedules represent another means for encouraging college students to take less remunerative positions when they graduate.) Repayment through service--whether through loan forgiveness or income contingency--has several important points in its favor. Two are that debt burdens would no longer inhibit borrowers in making career choices and the range of useful social activities that college graduates perform would be greatly expanded.

Student Aid Packaging. Debates over the specifics of Pell Grants and student loans often neglect the issue of student aid packaging. The federal government has never had an explicit policy for how much total federal aid a student could receive or how its aid programs are packaged. Yet, how different federal aid programs are put together can have an enormous impact on their effectiveness.

One of the most frequently discussed packaging issues over the past decade is the notion of frontloading grants, that is, giving students a higher proportion of grants in their first and possibly second year of study. Frontloading would probably have a very positive effect on access, at least at community colleges and trade schools where students are concentrated in the first two years of study. But to the extent that grant funds would be diverted from students at four-year institutions, frontloading could have a negative impact on choice. More importantly, frontloading would probably detract from retention to the extent it would encourage students to enroll but not finish their course of study. Frontloading also seems unlikely to promote better quality.

Another packaging issue is whether the federal government should establish an overall limit on the amount of aid it provides, as was recommended by a bipartisan national commission in 1993. An aid maximum, I believe, would make the federal aid system more effective for several reasons. It would provide greater predictability in the federal aid process in that students would know how much total federal aid they can receive. It also would allow the federal government to set policies for how its aid was packaged.

For example, if policy makers want to frontload grants in the first year or two of study and require more borrowing in later years, or allow students to choose between loans and work-study, these tradeoffs would be more easily accomplished if some overall federal aid maximum existed. I would establish an annual aid maximum for undergraduates, starting at $10,000 with adjustments over time for inflation. (A very small percentage of students currently receive more than this amount of federal aid.) To the extent that I would not allow remedial students and short-term training participants to borrow, no aid maximum would be warranted. To the extent that graduate students would be eligible for only loans or possibly work-study, no overall maximum seems warranted for these students either.

Relying More on Institution-Based Approaches

Institution-based programs have been the poor stepchild of federal policy since the decision in 1972 to move toward a student-aid-based strategy. This is unfortunate in my view because, in some instances, provisions that seek to affect institutional behavior may prove to be more effective in achieving some commonly sought after goals. To this end, I suggest consideration be given to utilization of institution-based efforts in the form of student support services programs and performance-based incentives.

Student Support Services Programs. An important and underutilized vehicle for achieving federal postsecondary policy objectives is the Student Support Services programs. The same legislation in 1972 that began the shift to a student-aid-based strategy ironically also reinforced the importance of the TRIO programs -- Upward Bound, Talent Search, and Student Support Services -- as a necessary complement to student aid.

TRIO-type programs often work well in helping academically at-risk students make a successful transition to college. They also can be critical in enabling disadvantaged students to complete their courses of study in a timely way. Given existing budgetary constraints, however, students in vocational training should not be participants in the TRIO programs. Instead, the TRIO programs should continue to be focused on helping at-risk students succeed in academic programs, including those students requiring remediation, who can most benefit from TRIO-type student support services.

The TRIO programs currently serve only a small fraction of the eligible population. Thus, perhaps the biggest question associated with a greater reliance on TRIO and other support services programs involves "going to scale," that is, how does a program move from a demonstration project basis to one that funds a much broader range of institutions.

Performance-Based Funding of Institutions. I believe that performance-based funding of institutions holds great potential for increasing retention and improving the quality of students and institutions. Institutional incentives for retention do not currently exist in the federal set

71

of programs. But, a number of states provide incentives in one form or another for institutions, both public and private, to graduate more students. Perhaps the federal government would do well to take a page out of the states' book.

Performance-based contracting would seem to work best for those types of postsecondary education and training in which the results are relatively easy to measure. (In many cases, technology-intensive approaches may work best with these students since so much of the learning can be accomplished through computer-based learning and the results are easily measurable.)

As noted earlier, I would not allow students in remedial programs to borrow and would replace loans with performance-based contracts with the various organizations that provide remedial courses, including community colleges, trade schools, high schools, and community based-organizations as well as a growing number of four-year colleges. The amount that providers receive would be tied to the reasonable costs of providing that remediation.

These contracts should be structured to reward those providers who get the best results at the lowest cost. To participate, providers would agree not to charge tuition to students for the remedial courses. As mentioned previously, need-based grants should be provided to the economically disadvantaged students to help defray at least some of their living costs while they are enrolled in remedial courses.

Performance-based contracts also should be considered as a replacement for loans for participants in short-term vocational programs. As in the case of remedial programs, short-term vocational training seems well-suited to performance-based contracts. Unlike the proposed remediation program, however, performance-based contracts for short-term training should be administered by the states in conjunction with the Department of Labor, since they are more aware than the federal Department of Education will be of local and regional labor market needs.

Federal incentives for retention should also be considered for addressing the problem of falling completion and graduation rates in academic programs. Rather than trying to address this problem through the student aid programs, perhaps more could be accomplished by providing incentives for institutions to graduate more of their economically disadvantaged students. For example, a portion of Pell Grant funding could be set aside to make payments to institutions on the basis of the number of Pell Grant recipients who graduated. With such a program, it would not be surprising to discover higher graduation rates for these students over time. This might also have the beneficial effect of institutions paying more attention to the needs and progress of their Pell Grant recipients.

Utilizing Tax Provisions

The federal tax code traditionally has contained a number of provisions that confer tax benefits on college students and their families. These include allowing parents to continue to claim an exemption for their college-age children who enroll in college as well as allowing employee and employer deductions for tuition benefits. A tuition tax credit or deduction for college tuition expenses, either for students directly or their parents, could have an impact on college enrollment trends.

Tuition Tax Credits or Deductions. Periodically over the past thirty years tuition tax credits or deductions have been proposed to allow parents to deduct or receive a credit for the college tuition expenses of their children. Ironically, the creation of the Guaranteed Student Loan program in 1965, and a major expansion in 1978, were both efforts to derail tuition tax legislation that was then pending. (With hindsight, we might have been better off with a thoughtful tuition tax plan than with the pell mell growth of loans. No pun intended.) The Clinton Administration climbed onto this well-travelled bandwagon in 1995 with its Middle Class Bill of Rights legislation.

Most economists and policy analysts argue against tuition tax credits or deductions because of their regressivity and the likelihood that they will benefit most those whose behavior will be unaffected (dead weight loss), while underserved populations will benefit the least. But a well structured tuition tax *credit* (not a deduction) could be beneficial in that it would provide tuition relief in a less intrusive way than having parents fill out financial aid forms to qualify to borrow subsidized loans. To reduce the budgetary impact of such a tax provision, however, students who qualify for the tax credit should be ineligible for any loan subsidies and their parents should not be eligible to borrow in the federal PLUS program.

It is also important that tuition tax benefits not be restricted to the parents of traditional-age college students. Tax benefits should be extended to nontraditional students for their own tuition expenses, at least for those individuals with limited means. One way to accomplish this would be for the federal government to pay an additional amount to cover a portion of the tuition expenses of individuals who qualify for the Earned Income Tax Credit (EITC). The EITC has been an important instrument of federal tax and social policy for the past twenty years. Although it recently has come under (somewhat surprising) attack by the Republican majority in Congress, it remains probably the most effective federal tax provision for the working poor.

Adding a tuition benefit to the EITC would encourage full-time workers to take one or two courses to enhance their employability, an incentive that is virtually nonexistent in the current system. Expanding the use of the EITC to include tuition, I believe, would have a far greater impact on the behavior of these people than the more typical prescription of extending Pell Grants to less-than-half-time students.

Improving Federal Quality Control and Regulation of Institutions

Ultimately, efforts to improve the effectiveness of the federal aid programs must address the issue of how the federal government ensures that participating institutions are of adequate quality. Although these questions of quality assurance typically take a back seat to more glamorous policy considerations, they are extremely important to the future health of the federal student aid programs.

The same student aid philosophy of one size fits all students seems to infuse federal policies regarding institutions. The notion of differentiating policies for various groups of students should apply to how the federal government deals with institutions. The same set of rules and regulations for institutions that are performing well should not apply to those institutions whose performance is questionable at best. It also seems appropriate that non-profit institutions should be governed by a different set of rules than proprietary schools.

Changes in federal policies for policing institutions should work in two directions: first, in reducing the regulatory burden on institutions that are performing well; and second, in providing greater scrutiny and oversight of institutions that are not performing at an adequate level.

Providing Regulatory Relief. Much has been made of the increasing burdens on institutions to comply with a growing number of complex federal regulations. Much of this burden arises because the regulations that are used to govern the behavior of problem institutions apply with equal weight to mainstream institutions that are performing adequately or well. Many observers have suggested that the federal programs would work better if those institutions that perform well were provided with some relief from *pro forma* regulatory requirements. The Clinton Administration's efforts in this area seem to be moving in this desired direction.

Improving Oversight of Poorly Performing Institutions. The federal government has traditionally relied on the "triad" of accreditation, state licensure, and periodic federal program reviews to provide quality control of the institutions that participate in the federal student aid programs. The much maligned State Postsecondary Review Entities (SPREs) were created in 1992 because of the widespread belief that the triad was not working.

The need to ensure adequate quality of the institutions that participate in the federal aid programs is no less diminished with the recent apparent demise of SPREs. To gain greater public trust of the student aid process, it is critical that problem institutions be identified and prevented from perpetrating further abuses. A good first step is to identify problem institutions on the basis of objective measures of performance, as again seems to be the direction the Clinton Administration is moving.

Another important step is to reassess the traditional federal program review process, which requires large amounts of staff time and resources (neither of which is in abundance in an era of government restraint). The traditional federal policies assume a certain degree of trust that institutions are in fact reporting accurately the information requested of them. This presumption of trust has backfired on any number of occasions as evidenced by congressional hearings and media reports on instances of fraud and abuse.

Rather than continue to rely on this program review process, the federal government should revise how it determines whether institutions are reporting accurately. Instead of trust, the federal government should adopt businesslike quality control procedures that assume a certain amount of fraud and deceit in the system. Institutions would then be periodically audited, with an oversampling of problematic categories of institutions, to determine whether the information they reported is accurate.

Concluding Remarks

The basic point of this paper is that federal policy makers need to think beyond student aid to mechanisms that may be more effective for certain groups of students. Federal policies also need to get beyond the notion that the same set of programs will serve all students equally well.

For undergraduates and graduate students, student aid should remain the primary vehicle of federal assistance. Collegiate and postbaccalaureate programs on average continue to pay high dividends in the form of increased earnings, and borrowing is a perfectly reasonable way to finance this investment. To clarify this correlation between loans and investment, I would restrict loans for undergraduates to the tuition and fees they pay up to a federal limit, and utilize grants and family resources to meet their basic living costs. To the extent many graduate students do not pay tuition and are not expected to rely on their parents for support, they should be able to borrow to meet living expenses.

Federal policies have run aground in the past when loans have been used extensively to finance activities in which the personal gain is less clear and much more uneven. In short, loans work best when the education and training that is being paid for is a good bet. For students requiring remediation and for participants in short-term vocational programs, therefore, alternatives to student loans should be employed to maximize the effectiveness of the federal investment. Performance-based contracting and other institution-based approaches hold promise for these types of postsecondary education and training in part because the results are much easier to measure than for undergraduates or postbaccalaureate students.

The federal system also ought to be more responsive to the needs of the non-traditional students who constitute a growing share of all college enrollments. Making an ongoing federal line of credit available to finance the multiple entries of these students into the postsecondary pipeline would seem like a good first step. Extending the Earned Income Tax Credit to pay for some college tuition expenses would be a good source of assistance for lower income workers taking a course or two to improve their employment prospects.

To ensure that the federal investment yields high returns, it also is necessary to improve the quality control exercised by the federal government on the institutions that participate in the federal programs. One element of this strategy should be to identify institutions that are not performing well and to institute business-based quality control techniques to better detect instances of fraud and abuse. The other aspect of this strategy should be to provide regulatory relief for those institutions that are performing well, thus freeing them up to do their job of educating and training millions of Americans every year.

Arthur M. Hauptman is an independent public policy consultant specializing in higher education finance issues. He also currently serves as a Senior Fellow of the Association of Governing Boards.

Starting Points: Fundamental Assumptions Underlying the Principles and Policies of Federal Financial Aid to Students

D. Bruce Johnstone

Federal financial aid to students in postsecondary education totals well over $30 billion, the majority of which is in the form of loans. Of the 18.5 million undergraduates enrolled full and part time during the 1992-93 academic year, more than six million received some form of federal student aid. The basic authorizing legislation is the Higher Education Act of 1965, as amended by periodic reauthorizations. In between these reauthorizations, politicians, policy analysts, and practitioners spend a great deal of time analyzing, bemoaning, and proposing alternatives to the voluminous statutory and regulatory language and the complex array of federal, state, and institutional participants involved in dispensing this assistance.

These discussions are frequently carried out amid a backdrop of self- and program-castigation. The programs are said to be ("as everyone knows") "a failure".... "unworkable"..."in need of total restructuring." This paper will argue an alternative viewpoint: that the programs are quite workable, and even quite sensible, *given several fundamental assumptions about the American higher education system that seem not to be on the table.* If something is genuinely and fundamentally wrong with the current pattern of programs, then there must be one or more things wrong with these fundamental assumptions. Conversely, if we are not to change any of these very fundamental assumptions, then it may be more productive to acknowledge the essential inevitability, if not necessarily the simplicity or the managerial elegance, of the current admittedly-complex pattern of programs, and to continue to perfect them "at the edges," with less distracting noise from those who would trash the whole process and have us begin again.

What are these fundamental assumptions of which the current "system" is such a logical (if complicated) outgrowth? I would propose the following seven:

1. Higher education is the province of the states, not of the federal government.

This point, like most that follow, might seem glaringly obvious. And yet, far too much of the time at this and dozens of other national conferences and congressional hearings will be taken up fussing about the proper workings of institutions that are simply not the federal government's to run--or even, other than the very important provision of financial aid to students (see #3 below) and the support of basic research, the business of the federal government. If it should be shown that the federal government's chosen role in the funding of higher education is having an unintended dysfunctional consequence, then the policy or procedure must be changed. But the most commonly alleged such consequence--that federal financial assistance to students contributes to profligate spending and thus to excessive tuition growth--is demonstrably nonsense. In short, although there may (or there may not) be serious managerial and other cost-side problems in higher education that are amenable to public policy solutions, these solutions are almost certainly not federal.

2. The costs of higher education are appropriately shared by taxpayers (both state and federal), parents, students, and philanthropists.

Other assumptions are possible, as attested by the experiences of other nations. In Scandinavia, for example, parents are not expected to contribute to the higher education costs incurred by their children. In the United Kingdom until only recently, students were not expected to contribute. In fact, for a system of highly accessible, mass higher education, the United States generates more revenue from other-than-taxpayer sources than any other nation.

By the U.S. assumption of shared costs, parents are assumed to be responsible, up to the limit of their ability to pay, for a portion of the costs of undergraduate education, or until the child-student has reached the age of 24 or 25 (give or take a few years). An upper limit is reached when parents are no longer willing to sacrifice, and when opportunities for their children are thus significantly curtailed. Students are also assumed to be responsible, through summer and term-time earnings and indebtedness, for a portion of the costs of their higher education, including the considerable costs of student living. An upper limit would begin to be reached on this share either when access begins to be significantly impaired, or when major life choices (e.g., marriage or choice of occupation) begin to be significantly impacted by indebtedness.

3. The role of the federal government/taxpayer in the financial support of the general instructional costs of undergraduate higher education has been to make up, through grants and loan subsidies, what low and low-middle income families can neither afford, nor are able or willing to borrow, in order to bring at least moderate-tuition, state-supported public education within reach of any student who is willing also to contribute himself or herself through term-time and summer earnings and loans. The federal government/taxpayer also makes student loans widely available, and in sufficient amounts, to bring higher-priced private education within reach for the student whose parents have contributed up to a reasonable limit, often with considerable indebtedness or depletion of assets, who are also willing to assume a substantial student indebtedness.

The federal government/taxpayer has thus chosen to support the principle of widespread access to undergraduate education through fully portable, need-based grants to undergraduates in sufficient amounts to bring low-tuition public higher education within reach of students who are also willing to contribute to their own college costs, through work and loans, but whose parents cannot reasonably be expected to contribute anything to the costs of their children's higher education. The only truly major alternatives for the federal government would seem to be either to leave the arena of basic undergraduate higher educational support altogether, or to revisit and reverse the profoundly significant decision of the early 1970s to *not* aid institutions directly, but to aid the enterprise of undergraduate higher education indirectly, through portable aid to students, and thus to support both institutions and access through the presumably benign workings of a competitive higher educational marketplace.

4. *The extent of state support of publicly owned colleges and universities (and thus the level of public tuition charged to parents and students in order to lessen the state taxpayer burden), in addition to any decision to subsidize private sector alternatives, either directly to institutions or indirectly through additional portable aid to students, are public policy decisions appropriately made at the state level.*

It follows from this assumption that federal financial aid is not meant to alter substantially the public-private sector balance that has emerged through the interplay of history, the preferences of students and families, and state public policies. This is why the Pell Grant has been essentially non-tuition sensitive, but why the federal government has increased unsubsidized loan limits, at minimal cost to the federal taxpayer, to be particularly accommodating to the higher-tuition private sector.

5. *Federal aid to students is given without regard to academic promise or performance.*

This assumption, qualified mainly by the federal aid requirement for "reasonable progress," is consistent with the primacy of need-based over merit aid, and also with the principle of encouraging very easy entry into the postsecondary system, but with considerable academic "weeding," as it were, taking place through almost continuous course-centered evaluations. The alternative would be federal aid that effectively denied aid, and thus denied (or at least discouraged) entry altogether to the children from low-income families who did not test well. The resulting differences or discriminations--by class, ethnicity, gender, region, or whatever--would be enormously divisive, as would any system of quotas or preferences erected to ameliorate against such distinctions.

6. *Federal aid to undergraduates, with few exceptions, is given without regard to course of study or intended occupation.*

In the United States the decision of major field of undergraduate study is left to the student and is assumed to be properly a function of his or her interest, aptitude, perception of job opportunities, and acceptance or aversion to uncertainty and risk. The alternative would be for the federal government to enact a national manpower policy, rewarding study only in those fields for which the federal government projected job opportunities or otherwise determined there to be a national need for graduates. However, manpower planning has proven to be so ineffective throughout the world, and so clearly contrary to the American fondness for individual occupational and economic freedoms, that it is not a likely course of U.S. policy, certainly not for the dispensing of general undergraduate student assistance.

7. It follows from assumption #2 (that students are to bear a share of higher educational costs) and assumption #5 (that financial assistance is to be made available to all who might reasonably seem able to perform college-level work) that student loans must be made generally available, without requirements of collateral, co-signature, or risk-rating. It further follows, then, that government must be the guarantor against the risk of default.

All other terms and conditions of student lending--rates, terms, provisions for subsidization, methods of repayment (e.g., income contingent, graduated payment, equal installment, who or what entities originate and/or service the loans, etc.) are legitimate matters for the Congress and for groups like this one to consider and reconsider. The only variation of considerable policy significance, for two reasons, is the degree of interest subsidization. The first reason is that high subsidies cost taxpayers money and thus can be considered a trade off for other forms of taxpayer-born student assistance. The second reason is that excessive subsidies on student loans require expensive and complicated means-testing to prevent excessive borrowing and credit disintermediation.

This is not meant to argue for a Panglossian best-of-all-possible-worlds approach to our current complex and not-inexpensive Title IV federal financial aid programs. But the problems of our federal student assistance programs remain both large and complex in part because we have chosen to graft a program of federal aid onto a higher educational enterprise that features:

- more than 1,600 public institutions, some of them with state constitutional autonomy and most of them with the relative autonomy (compared to other state agencies) of public corporations;

- some 2,000 private institutions, with all of the strange and sometimes messy governance characteristics of all higher educational institutions, plus the additional autonomy from governmental regulation enjoyed by private not-for-profit corporations; and

- nearly 7,000 postsecondary vocational and technical institutions, many of them private proprietary corporations, with all of the complexities cited above plus the powerful and sometimes problematic incentives of a dominant profit motive.

We have chosen as a nation, mainly at the state level, to support large systems of public higher education, and yet to maintain, encourage, and even publicly support an extensive array of private institutions. Some of them are among the most prestigious in the world, but very many of them are mainly entrepreneurial, with virtually open-admissions, and of little or no scholarly reputation.

We have chosen as a nation to embrace mass higher education--and furthermore to attempt to compensate for a long history of insidious racial discrimination and also (for complex social and economic factors) for a very large number of children born not only into deep poverty but also into dysfunctional families and neighborhoods, and neighborhood schools.

So why are we surprised that our federal financial aid "system" is complicated? It is, I would argue, overwhelmingly a reflection of the size and complexity of the higher educational enterprise itself and of the multiplicity and complexity of the social and institutional objectives that the system tries legitimately and purposefully to serve.

All too frequently, we react to the fact that the last HEA reauthorization in 1992 failed to restructure fundamentally the Title IV programs with the conclusion that "we" (the Congress, or the Department of Education, the financial aid profession, or the policy analysts) failed. Perhaps, instead, we should conclude that the programs are neither so odd nor so unworkable after all.

In conclusion, even if we were building from scratch a system of federal financial support to higher education that would make higher education accessible at the point of entry to most of our youth, that would avoid the slippery slopes of institutional micro-management or national curricula, that would support institutions but only indirectly through the support of students, thus encouraging a lively and competitive higher education marketplace; and that would maximize the cost-effectiveness of the federal dollars used in pursuit of these multiple objectives, then we would devise a system that would look very much like our current array of Title IV programs--even to the point of subsidized and non-subsidized loans, direct lending, multiple repayment options, and some participation for state agencies.

Bruce Johnstone is professor of higher and comparative education in the Department of Educational Organization, Administration, and Policy in the Graduate School of Education, University of Buffalo. Previously he served as Chancellor of the State University of New York, and has written and taught extensively in the area of higher education economics and finance.

Accountability in Postsecondary Education

Charles E. M. Kolb

These are difficult days for America's nonprofits. Whether the issue is salaries paid to nonprofit executives or congressional attempts to limit the efforts of nonprofits to lobby if they receive federal funds, there is little doubt that nonprofits of all types are facing greater public scrutiny than ever before. Part of the explanation is no doubt due to recent scandals: at United Way of America, Toys for Tots, the Foundation for New Era Philanthropy, and the NAACP.

Fraud and conspiracy allegations, along with charges of mismanagement, have a way of making waves not just with regulators and law enforcement authorities but, in the case of nonprofit charities, with the donor public as well. Not all of this increased oversight, however, is the result of individual wrongdoing. Although the scandals make interesting front page reading, the long term effect is really more substantial, part of a growing trend in the nonprofit world that can be called an "age of accountability." And like it or not, this trend is here to stay and will have profound consequences over the next decade on all nonprofits, but it can be expected to have a significant impact on one nonprofit group: postsecondary education institutions.

The scandals mentioned above are of relatively recent vintage and have played significant roles in sparking increased regulatory and law-enforcement activities. But it was another scandal -- one involving an institution of higher education -- that drew national attention to a case involving what probably struck some as little more than an accounting exercise: Stanford University's dispute with the federal government that broke in 1991 over the use of indirect cost rates and the misexpenditure of federal research dollars by the university during the 1980s. The Stanford controversy was, in many respects, the beginning episode that brought the "age of accountability" to American postsecondary education in particular and to the nonprofit sector more generally.

The accountability trend facing today's nonprofits represents a "third wave" of accountability. The first wave of accountability washed over corporate America during much of the 1980s. Responding to shareholder demands, enhanced global competition, and cost-saving new technologies, thousands of American companies launched upon major restructuring that meant sizeable layoffs and flatter bureaucratic organizations. The result today from that first wave is enhanced productivity, higher profits, and a more competitive corporate environment in which critical response time, given the advent of desktop computers, is measured in seconds.

The next wave touched government. The Reagan Administration launched a rhetorical and, initially, a budgetary war against "Big Government," but a bipartisan consensus about the need for government reform did not actually emerge until near the end of the Bush

Administration and the beginning of the Clinton years. Books such as David Osborne's and Ted Gaebler's <u>Reinventing Government</u> (1992) provided the intellectual justification and practical rationale for Vice President Gore's government-reform efforts in the National Performance Review. Policy analysts like Elaine Kamarck, who left the Progressive Policy Institute to work on Gore's efforts, contributed the day-to-day execution of the Clinton Administration's reinvention efforts. The November 1994 congressional elections pushed the trend even further. With the new Congress that assembled in January 1995, there was a greater sense of ideological urgency on the part of many freshman congressmen who were determined to rein in government spending, tackle the deficit, and dismantle the Great Society's legacy program by program.

Nonprofits were relatively untouched by these first two waves: most nonprofits lack shareholders in the customary for-profit sense, and the proposed federal budget cuts of the 1980s were limited, causing little economic harm. Yet, beginning in the mid-1980s, issues of accountability were emerging in ways that would subsequently have a significant impact on education reform, particularly at the elementary and secondary level and ultimately for postsecondary education institutions as well.

The education-reform debate that emerged after the 1983 publication of <u>A Nation At Risk</u> involved arguments for structural reform that were, for the most part, driven by accountability concerns reinforced by spending figures. To put the argument simply: with American aggregate education spending at the elementary and secondary level the highest in the world and per student spending almost at the top (well above competitors such as Germany, Japan, and Korea), why were our students doing so poorly?

This apparent inverse correlation between spending and performance formed the heart and soul of the education accountability debate as it was initially framed by the Bush Administration. The intent was, quite literally, to reorient the public policy debate away from how much we were spending on education to how we could ensure better educational performance and accountability for solid results. One crucial issue at the Charlottesville Education Summit in September 1989, for example, was whether the resulting joint communique between George Bush and the nation's governors would include calls for greater federal spending or remain focused primarily on the need for national education goals. Bush wanted to stress performance, standards, and assessments, while many Democratic governors sought higher levels of federal spending. By and large, the goals process -- with its emphasis on achievement -- carried the day, but only after several tense hours of late-night negotiations between Bush officials and then Arkansas Governor Bill Clinton.

As the national education goals process evolved after Charlottesville, the Republican administration's agenda was to focus less on "inputs" and more on "outputs" -- solid measures of achievement accompanied by reliable national (not federal) standards. Although the goals process has recently become bogged down in bureaucracy or partisanship, the effort nonetheless made significant strides in introducing accountability to education -- at least at the elementary and secondary level.

This thumbnail sketch of elementary and secondary education reform is important, particularly as a contrast with what was happening at the same time in postsecondary education. For it is accurate to observe that the third wave of accountability has only recently begun to touch postsecondary education after lagging the elementary and secondary sector for several years -- and for some very interesting reasons.

During the years when William Bennett was Education Secretary (1985-88), federal postsecondary education policy focused principally on two issues: the cost of the various federal programs and escalating student loan defaults. Interestingly, this essentially budget-driven emphasis parallelled the input-driven fixation that both the Reagan and Bush administrations were trying to alter in the elementary and secondary education context. Bennett succeeded in placing the student loan default issue on the congressional and regulatory reform agenda principally due to the occasional lurid story of some welfare recipient who had been enticed to apply for a Pell Grant voucher or sign up to receive a guaranteed student loan at some fly-by-night proprietary school that was fraudulently bilking the system for millions of dollars.

Only tangentially, however, did the great default debate raise the more complex issue of accountability for institutional and student performance and quality. It did so indirectly and obliquely through a hotly contested assertion in the proposed federal default regulations that a high default rate was, in effect, a proxy for a poor, substandard, low-quality institution. The principal rhetorical focus behind this contention was on those trade schools with exceedingly high default rates.

For the first time, a major effort was made to link the number of student loan defaults with institutional quality. Many schools bristled at this characterization, arguing instead that high default rates were more appropriately linked with the sluggish economy, the (relatively) underprivileged backgrounds of some of their enrollees, or other factors. The schools didn't default, they argued, students did, and many schools contended that they should not be held accountable for their former students' failure to pay off their student loans. The alleged linkage was never proven conclusively but, for the first time, the issue of accountability for quality was beginning to stir in the postsecondary world.

The initial focus, as noted, had been on high-default institutions. But what about comparatively low-default institutions that were not proprietary in nature but that were nonetheless graduating students with low or marginal skills in basic subject areas? What about those schools whose students knew little of American or world history, and who could barely construct a literate sentence? Didn't such institutions exist and, if so, what could be done about them?

That important issue had never really been addressed until relatively recently. The student loan default agenda played itself out ultimately in a series of federal regulatory changes that within a few years helped lower the volume of defaults. And, of course, the most recent reauthorization of the Higher Education Act raised new concerns such as the idea George

Bush rejected -- and which Bill Clinton readily embraced -- of establishing a less convoluted and cumbersome loan program by replacing guaranteed student loans with direct loans. Once again, issues of quality were overshadowed by concerns about program mechanics and financing.

During much of the last decade, the debates about postsecondary education policy have remained essentially input-driven: How can we reduce defaults? By how many basis points can we reduce the interest subsidy on student loans? Would the value of the Pell Grant voucher increase or decrease? Would there be an income-contingent repayment plan? Would the in-school interest subsidy continue? Would a variety of federal grant and fellowship programs survive the budget ax?

The focus has primarily been on delivery mechanisms, expanded access, and cost. (For an excellent survey of these issues, see A. Hauptman, The Tuition Dilemma: Assessing New Ways to Pay for College (1990)). By and large, these issues -- major as they appeared at the time -- were the functional equivalent of the elementary and secondary sector's preoccupation with spending until the emergence of the national education goals process. In the meantime, the consumers of postsecondary education -- by and large uninitiated in these essentially arcane and complex issues -- had experienced a different aspect of postsecondary education: rapid cost escalation far beyond the rate of inflation.

While the federal regulators were motivated by growing default costs and examples of some trade schools ripping off the system by recruiting students directly from welfare lines, another impetus toward accountability emerged from postsecondary education consumers. More and more parents (and their children) were growing alarmed over the costs of going to college. Moreover, when they paid tuition exceeding $25,000 annually at some elite (and some not so elite) schools, they wanted some assurance that their children were going to learn something that ensured their employability and that they would receive a solid educational foundation. They did not want to pay Cadillac prices four years in a row only to receive Yugo performance.

There was, however, one big problem in asking these questions: except for those elite schools where the name alone purportedly justified "prestige pricing," how could anyone measure the value added of a college education? To this day, that question haunts many institutions of higher education and lies at the very heart of the third wave of accountability now touching American higher education. The sad fact is that we don't yet know the answer.

How does one know not only the value added of a college education but, more precisely, how does one determine the comparative value of the thousands of institutions of higher education in America? Traditionally the answer has been to rely on the various government-approved accreditation agencies around the country as offering some assurance of quality. But until recently the accrediting agencies themselves have been primarily input-oriented (mirroring their elementary and secondary counterparts) and offered little in the way of concrete evidence. The accrediting agencies and many institutions of higher education respond that such questions of comparative education performance cannot be answered in large measure due to the immense variety among American postsecondary institutions. The effort itself, they say, would be meaningless.

This answer has evidently not satisfied everyone, and even the federal government -- the accreditor-in-chief of the accreditation agencies -- recently recognized a new accrediting body, the American Academy for Liberal Education, that was begun in 1992 by scholars such as Edwin O. Wilson from Harvard, Jacques Barzun at Columbia, and Elizabeth Fox-Genovese from Emory. The American Academy was needed, according to Dr. Barzun, because "students haven't learned to think, and the leading universities are leading us down into a pit." (W. Honan, "A New Group Will Accredit Some Colleges," New York Times, August 6, 1995).

American postsecondary education in the postwar years, spurred in large part by the remarkable access afforded by the Servicemen's Readjustment Act (GI Bill), has become increasingly accessible to students at virtually every income level. There has been unrivalled access to an ever increasing array of opportunities and variety of courses, but that access has not always meant access to quality, particularly when it comes to basic reading and writing skills.

The American Academy's president, Jeffrey Wallin, states: "[o]ne-third of all college courses are remedial. The students come illiterate and leave unlearned. We're against the frivolity of higher education. The core curriculum is the basis of the liberal arts curriculum, and it's in disastrous shape." (New York Times, supra.) Wallin cites the example of one midwestern university with approximately 4,000 courses that can be considered as part of its core curriculum. This situation brings to mind the reported exchange between Ralph Waldo Emerson and Henry David Thoreau. When the former boasted that Harvard now taught all the branches of human knowledge, Thoreau reportedly quipped: "Yes, all the branches but none of the roots."

The new American Academy's approach is novel because it will require adherence to 17 standards, including course requirements in areas such as science, languages, the classics, philosophy, history, politics, economics, and math. (Id.) It is quite likely that within a few years, the existing traditional accreditation agencies will have incentives to follow suit, just as the elementary and secondary sector began (albeit reluctantly) to move from input-based measures to standard-driven performance indicators.

The trends and pressures facing American postsecondary education during the next decade are fundamentally similar to the accountability pressures that another big player in the nonprofit world -- namely, charities -- is facing. As of 1993, there were more than 575,690 organizations in the United States registered with the Internal Revenue Service as tax-exempt 501(c)(3)s eligible to receive deductible charitable contributions. Competition for those charitable dollars is increasingly fierce, and charities -- including many institutions of higher education -- can no longer take for granted the beneficence they have enjoyed in the past. More donors now want to know how their dollars are being spent, what impact their contribution is having in the community, and whether the charity is keeping its administrative overhead as low as possible. Donors now often enjoy abundant choice when they contribute and are exercising that choice to support concerns ranging from health and human service charities to environmental, arts, and other "niche-marketed" charities. Charities that don't measure up are increasingly taken to task by watchdog entities such as the National Charities Information Bureau and others that provide "accreditation" going beyond what the IRS confers with its 501(c)(3) imprimatur.

For institutions of higher education, the next decade will bring similar developments, and the pressures will come from the following trends:

- rival accreditation bodies -- such as the American Academy -- will emerge, bringing to the accreditation process a more outcome-based method;

- the tuition cost spiral -- if it continues -- will spark an even greater consumer demand for information about student and institutional performance;

- the waning of the baby boom bulge will mean even greater competition among existing institutions of higher education from a shrinking student population; and

- there will be continued pressure to reduce federal resources for the various grant, loan, and fellowship programs.

As a result of these forces, postsecondary institutions -- as their charity counterparts in the nonprofit sector -- will face competitive pressures that they should embrace rather than resist. Embracing change means candor and greater disclosure of the factors that constitute overhead and rising tuition costs. Schools will undoubtedly respond to these pressures in various ways. Some will resist; others will dissemble in efforts to avoid sharing information that consumers find critical in deciding among competing institutions.

We have already seen examples of several schools inflating their SAT scores and graduation rates as reported in college guides published by U.S. News & World Report, Money, Barrons, and Peterson's. According to a recent Wall Street Journal story, some schools reported one set of figures to the popular guidebook publishers while giving a different (e.g., lower) set to Moody's credit reporting services or to Standard & Poor's. (S. Stecklow, "Colleges Inflate SATs and Graduation Rates In Popular College Guidebooks," Wall Street

Journal, April 5, 1995). <u>Wall Street Journal</u> reporter Gary Putka writes that "[i]n their efforts to woo students, many colleges manipulate what they report to magazine surveys and guidebooks in order to inflate their standing in the rankings, which are used widely by parents and students to select schools." (G. Putka, "U.S. News Addresses Flaws In College Guide -- Sort Of," <u>Wall Street Journal</u>, September 7, 1995).

Still other schools have only recently begun to respond to competitive pressures by using professional marketers (a practice once found primarily among proprietary institutions) to recruit students to attend their institutions. (S. Stecklow, "Some Small Colleges Hire Recruiters to Get Bigger Freshman Class," <u>Wall Street Journal</u>, September 5, 1995).

Competitive pressures, higher costs, and unfavorable demographics all point to a future for postsecondary institutions that will be far different from the past thirty years. Postsecondary institutions will sooner or later have to address explicitly -- and in quantifiable, objective, and measurable ways -- questions asked about the value they bring to a student's education. Those institutions that try to resist the pressure by protesting that their schools are unique, special, and cannot be measured by a common set of goals, standards, or learning objectives will find themselves playing a losing hand.

Until the Stanford scandal broke in 1991, the critics of higher education performance in America were generally either confined to or dismissed as coming from conservative-leaning academics or "ideologues." Since the late 1980s, however, these critics have been gaining more mainstream attention and followers. The late Allan Bloom at the University of Chicago published <u>The Closing of the American Mind: How Higher Education Has Failed Democracy and Impoverished the Souls of Today's Students</u> (1987), which became a surprise bestseller. Charles J. Sykes wrote <u>Prof-Scam: Professors and the Demise of Higher Education</u> (1988) and <u>The Hollow Men: Politics and Corruption in Higher Education</u> (1990). A young Dartmouth graduate, Dinesh D'Souza, made the issue of political correctness on the campus both a best-selling topic and a conservative rallying point in <u>Illiberal Education: The Politics of Race and Sex on Campus</u> (1991). A year later, former Reagan Administration domestic policy adviser Martin Anderson published <u>Impostors in the Temple: American Intellectuals Are Destroying Our Universities and Cheating Our Students of Their Future</u> (1992).

All of these books levelled blistering attacks on the performance of American higher education that have now resonated deeply in the popular culture. Such critics can no longer be readily dismissed, in large part because tens of thousands of education consumers find that the criticisms resonate whenever they wonder what their children are getting -- or likely to get -- from tuition charges that have been growing faster than inflation, faster than medical costs, and faster than their own disposable income. Moreover, with the founding of the National Association of Scholars in 1987 and the National Alumni Forum in 1995, it was evident that the critics of postsecondary education could now be found in academia itself and among thousands of dedicated alumni. Some donors are now demanding greater accountability in exchange for their charitable contributions to schools: even Yale discovered, to its chagrin that the multimillion dollar grant from Lee Bass could be readily revoked when the University failed to live up to the terms of the gift.

One small indicator that many of these concerns had emerged as mainstream was a brief and failed effort in 1993 to launch a goals process for higher education similar to that for elementary and secondary education. The National Education Goals Panel, established after the Charlottesville Summit to monitor progress toward the national education goals, voted unanimously in the summer of 1993 to create a new examination intended to measure what college students had learned. While the test would not rank schools or students, it would be used to help establish standards for American colleges, according to the Wall Street Journal. ("U.S. Education Panel Plans a College Exam To Establish Standard," Wall Street Journal, July 28, 1993). Although that fledgling process went nowhere, it is highly likely that unless higher education manages to reform itself, we can expect to see a serious effort to establish a national (not federal) standard-setting and assessment process for American postsecondary education within a few years.

This process, when it occurs, will represent a flowering of the accountability concept in the context of higher education. In fact, given the sector's reluctance to embrace change (it is one of the last places in American life, for example, to continue the concept of tenure), it is also likely that postsecondary education may be the last corner of the vast American nonprofit sector to recognize the staying power and seriousness of the growing consumer demands for accountability.

Chester E. Finn and Theodore Rebarber, writing about education reform in the elementary and secondary sector in 1992, offered the following observations:

> For a long time we had construed education
> in terms of intentions and efforts, plans and inputs,
> institutions and services. As long as we spent enough,
> tried hard enough, and cared enough, we believed we
> would have a good education system. In recent years,
> however, we have been moving, albeit fitfully, to
> redefine education in terms of how much people actually
> learn....
>
> A preoccupation with results implies that someone
> must be held responsible for producing them. This, too,
> is not something that the education system, left to its
> own devices, was apt to impose upon itself.... [T]he
> press for accountability is a major component of the
> reforms that characterize American education today.
> Finn & Rebarber, Education Reform in the '90s at 179
> (1992).

While the context is clearly different, Finn and Rebarber could just as easily have been describing the situation now facing American postsecondary education over the next decade.

The changes discussed above will eventually come, and the entire sector will emerge far healthier and stronger than it is today. Businesses have been restructured. The American military is now leaner and more efficient that it was 20 years ago. Government is being reinvented today. We may also now be entering a time of intense "pruning" in the case of American higher education. The branches will probably be trimmed a good bit, but the roots will then dig deeper in order to provide even greater nourishment in the future.

Charles E.M. Kolb served from 1988 to 1990 as Deputy Under Secretary for Planning, Budget and Evaluation at the U.S. Department of Education. From 1990 to 1992 he was Deputy Assistant to the President for Domestic Policy at the White House. Mr. Kolb is an attorney with degrees from Princeton University, Oxford University (Balliol College), and the University of Virginia School of Law. He has been General Counsel at United Way of America since November 16, 1992.

Goals for Federal/State Policy in the 21st Century:
Affordability, Mobility and Learning Productivity

James R. Mingle

This paper suggests that the federal government, in partnership with the states, should organize programmatic and financial aid policies to achieve the following objectives: (1) assure affordable options for postsecondary education and training for all young people and adults; (2) improve the mobility of student learners to move across state lines to access postsecondary education, and promote the "mobility" of institutions to provide access through technology to place-bound students; and (3) improve the learning productivity of students by assisting them in achieving a higher level of skill and knowledge attainment in the most cost-effective manner. Each of these objectives is closely interrelated. Affordability can be sustained in part by matching demand with capacity regardless of location. Learning productivity, in the form of more purposeful enrollment and more rapid progression toward skill and degree attainment, can also contribute to affordability through a more effective use of scarce resources. Mobility and learning productivity are also linked through recognition that technology allows the delivery of educational services in an "anytime, anyplace" mode.

The paper assumes that these objectives cannot be met by action of the federal government alone but must be carried out in concert with state governments, which are the primary providers of public support for postsecondary education. The paper's proposals on student financial aid deal exclusively with joint federal/state partnerships for grant programs and assumes that the federal government will continue to provide access to loan capital through the Direct Lending program and the Guaranteed Student Loan program. Although the writer recognizes that the changes proposed would alter the accountability mechanisms employed by the federal government, this issue is not covered within the scope of this paper. Nor does the writer examine the implications of the proposed changes on independent nonprofit and proprietary institutions, important issues which will need further study.

Affordability

The net price, or cost, of an education to an individual student varies widely depending on the type of institution chosen, the income of the student and the income of the student's parents, as well as the availability of student aid. For the 11 million students who are enrolled in the public sector (80 percent of all students), affordability is most directly affected by the level of public sector tuition, fees, room and board charges, and the availability of federal, state, and institutional aid. Affordability also is affected by the ability of students and parents to meet these costs as reflected in their family income. A variety of authors and researchers have reported on the problem of affordability and its effects on student participation, debt burden, and persistence. (Gladieux and Hauptman, 1995;

Mortenson, 1994) The declining purchasing power of the Pell Grant, rising college costs, and the stagnant growth of family income combine to make college less affordable. In the case of public institutions, recent actions of state government and public boards of trustees have added to the affordability problem. Many states, often out of necessity, have abandoned their historical commitments to low public sector tuition. Students who once were paying 15-30 percent of total instructional costs may now be paying as much as 50 percent of these costs. This reflects not so much a change in philosophy as the press of other state budget priorities, such as health care and criminal justice, which have put pressure on tuition to offset cutbacks in state appropriations. Future efforts of the federal government to cut the deficit are likely to further erode the ability of states to maintain low tuition policies. Estimates place the cost of deficit reduction on the states as upwards of $30 billion by the year 2000. (Sheppach, 1995)

To offset a portion of these costs to students, states have over the years created their own need-based student aid programs. In 1993-94, the states spent about $2 billion on need-based aid (as compared to approximately $6 billion spent by the federal government). While all states have some type of program, the bulk of need-based aid is concentrated in a very small number of states. Seven states (New York, California, Illinois, Pennsylvania, New Jersey, Ohio, and Minnesota) account for 61 percent of the total aid awarded (NASSGP, 1994). Although state support for need-based aid has grown in recent years, it appears that these increases have not been great enough to cover the increases in costs to students. The College Board, for example, reports annual tuition increases in the public sector for 1991, 1992, and 1993 at 8.4 percent, 6.5 percent, 6.4 percent, respectively. NASSGP reports median increases for state aid for 1991, 1992, and 1993 at 3.8 percent, 6.4 percent, and 3.2 percent respectively.

Principles for a New Federal/State Partnership

If these trends continue, affordability of college among lower and middle income students may become severely threatened. The result will be growing indebtedness and falling participation and completion rates. In order to counter this drift, the federal government, in partnership with states, will need to take positive steps to insure affordability. This paper argues that by using federal grant dollars as leverage, affordability can be sustained through state commitment to hold public sector costs down or to assure that need-based aid compensates for the growth in costs. The alternative to this approach appears to be for the federal government to try and sustain the purchasing power of its grant programs in response to independent pricing actions by the states, a daunting task to say the least.

One of the striking features of the current federal/state partnership in financing postsecondary education is its inconsequential nature. The two entities — federal and state — essentially operate on separate tracks. The federal government establishes its policies with no coordination with, or influence on, state entities. States, in response to their own political and economic determinants, directly set, or indirectly influence, the price charged for attendance at public institutions. A similar lack of coordination often takes place at the state level as institutional aid, tuition and fee policy, and student aid appropriations often respond to different dynamics. Few states have attempted, for example, to make up for the declining purchasing power of the Pell Grant or have sought to moderate tuition in response to cutbacks in federal aid. Nor have state actions had much influence on federal policy.

This paper proposes to change this two-track policy setting. It establishes principles for the coordination of state pricing policy with federal aid policy. It starts with the assumption that the setting of tuition and other costs by a state or an institution is the determining variable in the equation. Influencing that pricing decision and subsequent state actions should be an important (but not the only) goal of federal policy. At the same time, federal policy should be carried out in such a manner as to ensure the flexibility of states to take different paths to the same end — affordability. Some states will continue to choose the "low tuition" route; others may decide to raise tuition and increase their commitment to need-based aid. The federal government should maintain its current commitment to need-based aid but use that aid in a way either to keep tuition costs down or to increase state commitment to need-based aid.

Improving Affordability through a "Super SSIG"

In 1993-94, the State Student Incentive Grant Program (SSIG) provided $72 million in federal dollars as an incentive for states to invest in student aid. Requirements for participation in the program include minimal incentives for "maintenance of effort." For many large states, it is an inconsequential program since these states have long ago "overmatched" the program with their own substantial state aid programs. The state of New York, for example, receives $6 million in federal SSIG funds, while providing about $600 million in state funds (a 100 to 1 match). In other states, the federal program is a more substantial portion of the total need-based effort. Seven states, for example, provide only the minimal one-to-one match required in the program and another seven provide only a three-to-one match. The small size of this federal program and its relatively modest contribution to states has made the program vulnerable to federal cuts and calls from both Republican and Democrat administrations for elimination.

This paper proposes the creation of a new "Super SSIG" that would combine all existing federal need-based grant programs into a partnership program with the states. The Super SSIG would have the following characteristics:

- It would subsume the current Pell Grant program, campus-based programs, and SSIG into a $6 billion-plus state "block" grant program.

- Federal allocation formulas to the states would be based on income and college participation factors.

- State eligibility factors would be based on a state meeting a specified proportion of student costs among eligible students. As tuition and other college costs rise, a state would be forced to increase its commitment to grant aid. As a state's population of "needy" students rises, the federal government's allocation to the state would grow.

- State eligibility for federal block grants also would depend on the full portability of the state portion so that students could use these funds at all eligible institutions regardless of state location (e.g., at all regionally accredited institutions).

Table 1 presents a hypothetical scenario for a federal/state grant formula. In State A, a high tuition state, college costs to the student are $6,000, to which the federal and state governments combined have committed to cover 70 percent of these costs. In the base year, the state's obligation for need-based grants is set at $13.9 million. In year two, the state decides to increase its tuition or other costs to students by $200. (The number of eligible students remains the same.) In order to remain eligible for the continuing federal grant, the state is obligated to increase its appropriation by an equal amount, in this case 3.3 percent.

In State B, a low tuition state, the base year obligation of the state is $6.9 million, which earns the state an additional $14.1 million federal block grant. In year two, the state decides to increase its tuition by $1,000 which obligates the state to increase its need-based aid funds by 33 percent in order to maintain its eligibility for federal funds. In this illustration, the federal government has limited the growth in its obligation to 3 percent, plus the additional costs of financing 200 new eligible students. This action results in a shortfall of $4.3 million (unmet need). Given that the increases in tuition will be paid by all students, not just those receiving aid discounts, the state may decide to maintain or even increase its share of total costs. If the state does not, the share borne by students will need to be increased. Falling below a minimal share of state support could put eligibility for federal funds at risk. A reciprocal obligation would exist on the part of the federal government. Failure to maintain its commitment would free the state from its obligations as well.

Table 1
Determining State and Federal Shares for
the "Super SSIG" Program:
Two Hypothetical Cases

	Student Costs	Eligible Students	Total Costs (in millions)	Gov't Share	Total Need (in millions)	Federal Share	State Share	State Obligation (in millions)	% Increase	Federal Obligation (in millions)	% Increase	Unmet Need (in millions)
State A Year 1	$6,000	10,000	$60	0.7	$42	.067	.033	$13.9		$28.1		
State A Year 2	$6,200	10,000	$62	0.7	$43.4	0.67	0.33	$14.3	3.3%	$29.1		
State B Year 1	$3,000	10,000	$30	0.7	$21	0.67	0.33	$6.9		$14.1		
State B Year 2	$4,000	10,200	$40.8	0.7	$28.6	0.67	0.33	$9.2	33.3%	$15.1*	7.1%	$4.3

* 3% increase over Year 1 plus $618,000 for new students (Year 1 tuition x 1.03 x 200 new students)

In this model, the state decision on tuition and other college costs is the determining variable. States choosing to maintain low tuition or modest increases would be rewarded with continuing eligibility for federal dollars and proportional increases in federal support. States choosing to increase tuition significantly would face commensurate obligations to increase state grants. If those increases exceeded caps on growth in federal funds, the state could choose to lower the share of need met by governmental support or use the additional revenue generated by tuition increases to maintain the 70 percent share.[1]

An alternative approach to the Super SSIG would be aimed at changing the relative mix of federal and state contributions to aid. Instead of subsuming the current Pell Grant program, the current SSIG might be expanded significantly, say to a $1 billion annual appropriation. States with only modest commitments to need-based aid would be required to increase significantly their commitment (over time) in order to maintain eligibility. States would continue to set standards for need and eligibility as they currently do for SSIG funds, but maintenance of effort formulas would be aimed at accelerating the match. Some have suggested that the current ratio of three dollars of federal grant money to one dollar of state money be changed so that in future years, the ratio might be changed to three to two or two to one by increasing state commitments to need-based aid. The problem, however, is illustrated by comparing the current federal-to-state matches in two states, New York and Alabama. In the former, the $700 million in federal grant support is matched by $600 million in state support. In Alabama, the $135 million in federal support is matched by only $1 million in state support.[2]

From the federal perspective, this would be a powerful incentive to make up for some of the proposed cutbacks in federal aid. From a state perspective, especially among states with

---

[1] In 1991, Michael McPherson and Morton Shapiro, in a book entitled *Keeping College Affordable*, proposed a series of changes aimed at a similar objective of influencing state tuition setting behavior. Based on the annual instructional cost of an education at a public two-year community college, McPherson and Shapiro proposed a maximum $5,800 grant for needy students. This, they reasoned, would push states to increase dramatically tuition in the public sector in order to fully capture the federal largesse. Their objective was to make the federal government assume greater responsibility for students of need while allowing states to use the additional tuition revenue to enhance institutional support. In contrast, the Super SSIG proposal asks the states to increase their commitment to grant aid only in proportion to increases in college costs. It assumes that the states, not the federal government, will be the primary determinants of affordability. It further assumes that the federal government commitment to grant aid will remain limited in the foreseeable future.

[2] These comparisons are taken from data provided by the National Association of Student Financial Aid Administrators and include Pell Grant, SEOG, Federal Work-study, and federal SSIG contributions.

relatively small aid programs (and relatively low tuition), this could be viewed as a heavy-handed federal intrusion.

The Development of Education Trust Accounts: This is an idea that could be combined with the Super SSIG. The establishment of education trust accounts for all school-age children was proposed by McGuinness in 1992 and Armajani, Heydinger and Hutchinson in 1994. Such education trust funds might include state savings plans, service earnings and credits prepayment plans and other vehicles for individual contribution. Upon determination of eligibility for need-based grants, the state and federal governments would credit the individual account and the institution carrying the enrollment would make withdrawals. One of the side benefits of such accounts would be considerable simplicity and regulatory relief for institutions. Changes in federal and state policies as to eligibility and need would be handled by the state agencies, not institutional financial aid offices. Additional federal and state appropriations would need to be obtained in order to establish the endowment funds for future generations. (This approach is similar to the "I Have A Dream" programs upon which the current early intervention initiatives of the federal government are based.)

Evaluating Future Proposals: Given the current budget-cutting climate in the Congress, there may be a variety of future proposals which, in a similar fashion to welfare reform, will seek to off-load federal responsibilities to the states through block grants. This is clearly not the intent of this proposal. This writer would suggest the following criteria for judging the value of state/federal partnership programs: (1) the degree to which they maintain and, if possible, increase the commitment of both the federal and state governments to need-based grants; (2) the degree to which they provide flexibility at the state level in maintaining either low tuition/low aid or high tuition/high aid strategies; and (3) the degree to which they contribute toward the goal of affordability.

Achieving Greater Mobility of Students and Institutions

In contrast to European countries, which are moving toward reciprocity, American state governments are systematically placing barriers to the movement of students across state lines. Many states have adopted policies that out-of-state students in public institutions must pay 100 percent or greater of the cost of education. Restrictive residency laws also reduce the free flow of "education commerce." Moreover, the distribution and utilization of postsecondary institutions varies widely across the country. Growing states along the "southern tier" and in the Pacific Northwest and mountain states are pressed to find room for their own residents, while states with stable or declining populations in the northeast and upper midwest have institutions which are desperate for new enrollments. The result is a national mismatch between supply and demand.

The residency and tuition policies of states can result in both provinciality as well as irrational subsidy policies that work against the best interests of both individuals and states. Take, for example, the state of Colorado, which is experiencing considerable in-migration from other states, especially California. A recent in-migrant with college-age children immediately becomes eligible, independent of need, for a significant state subsidy to attend a Colorado public institution. That in-migrant may have contributed little or nothing to the state tax base that pays this subsidy, and his children, given the current mobility of the population, may not spend much of their subsequent working life in the state. At the same time, an out-of-state applicant who applies, for example, to the popular Boulder campus of the University of Colorado, will pay tuition rates set at 120 percent of educational costs and receive no state subsidy, even though that person may well spend the rest of his or her working life in the state. Moreover, that California applicant may have been motivated to apply to the University of Colorado, Boulder, because of the lack of space in a comparable California institution.

In a 1994 seminar at the Brookings Institution, Gordon Davies, director of the State Council of Higher Education for Virginia, cited the expected growth in his state as a reason for supporting portable state aid. "This would attack two problems at once, one being student need and the other, how we (in the South) handle a tremendous amount of enrollment growth. Maybe it is that last piece (mobility) that makes [the Super-SSIG] attractive." (Gladieux and Hauptman, 1995, p.116)

From a national perspective, promoting the free flow of students across state lines has the same advantages that led the founding fathers to prohibit the states from disrupting the flow of commerce across state lines. In fact, the application of the "interstate commerce" clause has some applicability to tuition and residency laws in the states as noted by a recent ruling of a federal district court in Michigan. (U.S. Court of Appeals, 1994) By acting as a counterforce to the natural inclination of states to reserve subsidies for "their residents," the federal government can be a powerful force for maximizing the effective use of existing institutions and by encouraging students and their parents to be able to match their education decision making with the national realities of the job marketplace.

Bringing the "Campus" to the Student: In recent years, "mobility" has taken on a new meaning. The federal government should be a force for promoting not only the mobility of students to institutions but also of institutions to students. The emerging national and global digital networks, which can transmit voice, video, and data not only to remote sites but also to the desktop in a student's home and office, already is spawning a host of new and traditional providers to deliver instruction to distant sites.

One of the characteristics of these emerging networks is that they show no respect for political boundaries. Already new consortia of existing institutions or whole new entities are offering courses, and sometimes complete degree programs, to national and international markets. This can be done over fiber optic cable and telephone lines that connect computers and video equipment to vast networks of information, data, and instructional programs. Add to this emerging electronic highway existing cable systems and satellite delivery systems and you have an enormous network open to educational programming.

100

The options open to students are likely to expand exponentially in the years ahead, especially for working adults and place-bound students. This will create both opportunity and problems for policy makers. Students, for example, who already collect credits from three or four or five institutions in their academic career, may be collecting credits from dozens of institutions, compounding the problem of articulation and certification of credit and mastery.

For the most part, states and individual institutions, both public and independent, have taken a "protectionist" attitude about subsidizing providers. While their own state institutions may be engaged in electronic-based distance education, state policy makers and in-state operators are likely to be suspicious of the quality of out-of-state providers and seek through regulation and subsidy policies to limit their access to state residents. In some cases, they may be right. Technology developments may open the door even wider for diploma mills to take advantage of unwary students. But at the same time, these developments hold tremendous potential for extending access to place-bound students and of empowering consumers to seek high quality offerings that meet their needs. It is this tendency that the federal government should support through its own subsidy policies and grant-making activities.

There are a number of ways in which the federal government can promote both mobility of students across state lines and mobility of institutions to operate independent of political boundaries. The federal government should consider:

1. Implementing the "Super SSIG" program, discussed earlier, with its requirement of portability to all accredited institutions, regardless of location.

2. For purposes of student aid eligibility, treating enrollment in courses that are conducted at a distance or in asynchronous mode in the same fashion as traditional residential enrollments.

3. Requiring (or encouraging) accrediting bodies to establish "standards of good practice" in distance learning in order to prevent low-quality fraudulent operators. The federal government might also increase its own "consumer information" activities to inform students of good practice in electronically-mediated instruction.

4. Encouraging the courts to examine state residency requirements in order to prohibit restraint of trade and promote the free flow of educational commerce across state lines.

5. Supporting through grant-making agencies the development of national and international networks of instructional delivery.

Learner Productivity

Student aid policy, while critically important, should not be the sole focus of federal policy toward higher education. Although the federal government has established an effective policy framework for supporting graduate education and research, there exists no comprehensive strategy aimed at improving undergraduate teaching and learning (with the notable exception of the Fund for the Improvement of Postsecondary Education). This paper argues that the Department of Education should undertake a concerted effort to improve the capacity of institutions and the motivation of students to engage in purposeful and effective teaching and learning. Without such a policy, student aid funds are likely to be used ineffectively. It is no longer sufficient to ensure access in accomplishing national goals in higher education. Students will need to improve their learning productivity for the nation to remain competitive in the world economy and for affordability for all to be sustained. The proposals outlined below shift the emphasis of public policy and support in important ways: first, by building the capacity of institutions to focus on learning; and second, by raising the standards, expectations, and motivations of students to assume greater personal responsibility for their own learning. The overarching goals of these strategies are summarized in the phrase "learning productivity," coined by Bruce Johnstone, former chancellor of the State University of New York. Johnstone referred to the goal of greater knowledge and skill attainment from larger proportions of the student population in a shorter period of time.

Building a National Learning Infrastructure: The task of building a "national learning infrastructure" is the task of the 21st century. Free of the paradigms of both teaching and research, such an infrastructure builds upon the emerging global computer and telecommunications networks. It puts learning tools — both hardware and software — in the hands of students and not only expands their choices and options but their learning productivity as well.[3]

The role of the federal government in building such an infrastructure is comparable to its role in supporting and sustaining a research infrastructure for higher education. Through its grant-making agencies it can support and spread the development of learning tools, especially among the "have-not" sectors of higher education. Here are a few examples of how this might be done:

---

[3] This vision of a national learning infrastructure is articulated best in the work of Educom, a national organization concerned with the application of information technology to higher education. See, for example, Heterick (1994), Graves (1994) and Twigg (1994). For more information on the National Learning Infrastructure Initiative (NLII) of Educom, contact NLII@Educom.edu or call the Educom Office, 202-872-4200.

1. Provide support for institutions to extend access to personal computers. A few cutting-edge institutions have concluded that the future of instructional technology lies with assuring that all of their students "own" their own personal computers (often laptops), which are connected to networked software and other services such as the Internet. The value of a personal computer already is widely recognized by those students and parents who can afford to purchase one, but the effect of all students having their own computer can be seen in those few public and private institutions that have mandated such ownership. The result could be nothing short of a complete transformation of the teaching/learning process. With the federal government carefully assisting institutions, especially those with large proportions of students on financial aid, it might well be able to operationalize the calls of Vice President Gore and Speaker Gingrich for greater access and utilization of technology. (Resmer, Mingle, Oblinger, forthcoming)

2. Support consortial development of high quality instructional software and multi-media programming. New consortia, such as the one led by Rennselaer Polytechnic to develop materials for undergraduate courses in physics (and a whole new delivery mode), are providing models for replacement of the "cottage industry" of curriculum development that characterizes much of higher education. A number of critical problems that are the key to learner productivity cry out for a consortial approach: for example, the development of learning materials in remedial mathematics and language acquisition. Such materials might be delivered over "distributed learning" networks with national protocols to aid in the easy use and access by faculty and students. Given the way in which markets for textbooks and other materials have been developed in the past, it may take federal support to stimulate research and development in this area. Technology-based curricula require greater capitalization and broader markets than the typical textbook development process. With modest support, consortia of institutions may be able to create these markets and define the standards needed to stimulate private sector investment.

3. Sponsor studies of the cost effectiveness of different delivery systems. Through such agencies as Office of Educational Research and Improvement, the federal government can support the careful study of the cost effectiveness of technology-based instruction. What mix of technology and faculty support produces the highest level of learner productivity at the least cost? It is a critical question if we are to achieve our goals of a learning society.

Establishing Higher Expectations and Standards: The second major thrust of the learning productivity goal should be to provide direct incentives for students to change their behavior and expectations. Too little attention has been paid to how student eligibility standards for financial aid might be altered to affect learner productivity. Through a judicious raising of standards of eligibility and through the placement of limitations on length of eligibility, students can be encouraged to improve their preparation for college and their motivation to succeed in a timely manner. At the same time, at-risk students who currently have high failure rates can be given the financial support to obtain base-line skills without incurring large amounts of debt. The following changes should be considered:

1. Increase the floor academic eligibility or "ability to benefit" standards for participation in federal student loan programs. Students taking remedial work should not be eligible for participation in student loan programs. Rather, they should be fully supported, if they demonstrate need, through federal and state grants. Such eligibility might be limited both as to number of remedial credits as well as time from initial enrollment. (See Hauptman, Mingle, 1994 for further discussion.)

2. Limit the number of credit hours that are subsidized through grant and loan programs. Some states have begun to place limits on the total number of credit hours receiving state subsidy as well as absolute caps on the credit hours that constitute a baccalaureate degree. Federal policy can support these developments by placing a credit hour limit on Pell Grant and loan eligibility. Such a move would not only support a cost-effective use of scarce student aid dollars but could also be a powerful motivator for students to engage in "purposeful" enrollment and thus shorten their time to degree.

James R. Mingle is executive director of the State Higher Education Executive Officers, a national organization of statewide coordinating and governing boards in Denver, Colorado. He is currently on leave as a visiting fellow with Educom, examining issues of state investment strategies for technology. Mingle received his Ph.D. from the University of Michigan and has served SHEEO as its director since 1984.

Bibliography

Armanji, Babak, Richard Heydinger and Peter Hutchinson. *A Model for the Reinvented Higher Education System*. Denver: State Higher Education Executive Officers, 1994.

The College Board, *Trends in Student Aid*. Washington, D.C.: The College Board, 1994. (Figures used are "cost of attendance, current dollars".)

Gladieux, Lawrence E. and Arthur M. Hauptman. "Improving Public Policies to Help Students Pay For College." Washington, D.C.: The Brookings Institution/The College Board. Draft manuscript, April 1995.

Graves, William H. "Toward a National Learning Infrastructure." *Educom Review*, Vol. 29. No. 2, March/April 1994.

Hauptman, Arthur M. and James R. Mingle. *Standard Setting and Financing in Post-secondary Education: Eight Recommendations for Change in Federal and State Policies*. Denver: State Higher Education Executive Officers, 1994.

Heterick, Robert C. "Reengineering Teaching and Learning." A Presentation to the CAUSE Annual Meeting, 1994. Available from jrudy@cause.colorado.edu or the Educom Offices, Washington, D.C.

McGuinness, Aims C., Jr. "Redesigning the States' Higher Education System for the 21st Century." Presentation at the ECS National Forum, Cincinnati, Ohio, August 7, 1992.

McPherson, Michael S. and Morton O. Shapiro. *Keeping College Affordable: Government and Educational Opportunity*. Washington, D.C.: The Brookings Institution, 1991.

Mortenson, Thomas G. "Restructuring Higher Education Finance: Shifting Financial Responsibility from Government to Students." Eleventh Annual Financial Aid Research Network Conference of NASSGP and NCHELP. San Francisco, California, April 7, 1994.

National Association of State Scholarship and Grant Programs. *NASSGP 25th Annual Survey Report: 1993-94 Academic Year*. Harrisburg, PA: Pennsylvania Higher Education Assistance Agency, May 1994.

National Association of Student Financial Aid Administrators. Data provided the author.

Resmer, Mark, James R. Mingle and Diane Oblinger. *Providing Universal Technology Access to Students*. Denver: State Higher Education Executive Officers, 1995.

Sheppach, Ray. Presentation to the State Higher Education Executive Officers, Washington, D.C., March 21, 1995.

Twigg, Carol A. "The Need for a National Learning Infrastructure." *Educom Review*, Volume 29, Number 5, September/October 1994.

U.S. Court of Appeals, 6th Circuit, Case No. 92-2424; 1994 APP0259P, 6th Circuit, File #94A0259P.06.

Pursuing Broader Participation and Greater Benefit from Federal College Student Financial Aid

Toward New Purposes, Guidelines and Requirements for a More Efficient and Effective College Student Aid Program

Michael T. Nettles
(with assistance of Catherine M. Millett and Laura W. Perna)

The Reform Idea

Introduction

Typically, historical analyses of federal financial aid policy begin with the Higher Education Act of 1965. Yet, if the analyses of the contemporary era of financial aid begin with the Serviceman's Readjustment Act of 1944 (the GI Bill), it is possible to examine not only the incubation of the broader 1965 financial aid policy but also to witness a time when the major national financial aid program was characterized by a single, clear policy with easy to understand eligibility requirements and administrative processes, as well as an impact which was easy to measure. In contrast to the GI Bill, which provided financial support for veterans who had performed honorable service for the country to attend college, today's financial aid policy includes a broad array of programs, each satisfying different purposes for different segments of the population who meet different thresholds of need.

A primary purpose of the federal financial aid programs authorized under Title IV of the Higher Education Act of 1965 is to ensure access and opportunity for students to attend college. Whether this has been accomplished is questionable. Several observers of higher education trends and financial aid have suggested that access has actually declined (Mortensen, 1991, and Orfield, 1992). In addition, the accumulation of numerous increases in the number and types of programs, modifications at different times to either expand or reduce eligibility for grants and loans, and alterations in the conditions for loan repayment, have resulted in disparate programs that lack coherence of purpose. Furthermore, fraud and abuse have become associated with the student loans program, which raises questions about the credibility and efficiency of national financial aid programs.

This paper outlines the expansion of federal financial aid policy, presents some of the challenges confronting the current federal financial aid policy, and proposes for consideration by the national government, a new policy direction aimed at increasing the efficiency and effectiveness of federal financial aid expenditures. The paper concludes with several policy questions that need to be addressed in order to monitor the effectiveness of the national policy.

Expansion of national financial aid policy

Since the enactment of the GI Bill, federal financial aid policy has grown to include the National Defense Student Loan program of 1959 (renamed first the National Direct Student Loan program and then later the Perkins Loan program); the College Work-Study program and the Educational Opportunity Grant program (now called the Supplemental Educational Opportunity Grant), both of which were established through the Civil Rights Act of 1964 and subsequently incorporated into the Higher Education Act of 1965; the Guaranteed Student Loan program (now called the Federal Family Education Loan program) which was established under the Higher Education Act of 1965; and the Basic Educational Opportunity Grant program (renamed the Pell Grant in 1980).

Figure 1 shows that today, the federal government is by far the most important source of student financial assistance, contributing roughly 75 percent of all aid ($31.43 billion of the total $41.94 billion) provided to college students in academic year 1993-94 (The College Board, 1994). The magnitude of financial aid for college students is evident by the fact that financial aid for college students comprises over two-thirds of the annual appropriation to the U.S. Department of Education (The Digest of Education Statistics, 1994).

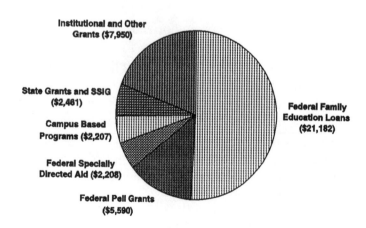

Figure 1
Estimated Student Aid by Source: Academic Year 1993-94
(Current Dollars in Millions)

Institutional and Other Grants ($7,950)

State Grants and SSIG ($2,461)

Campus Based Programs ($2,207)

Federal Specially Directed Aid ($2,208)

Federal Pell Grants ($5,590)

Federal Family Education Loans ($21,182)

Despite its favorable legacy of providing access and opportunity for disadvantaged citizens to attend college, the growth in financial aid policy has been accompanied by greater scrutiny and discontent. Evidence of the Congress' dissatisfaction with the program is revealed through the following actions:

- including new provisions in the 1992 Higher Education Reauthorization Act regarding integrity in the financial aid policy, such as auditing and reporting requirements for colleges and universities and the establishment of State Postsecondary Review Entities (SPRE);

- decreasing the rate of growth in appropriations, causing annual declines in the purchasing power of financial aid awards that students receive;

- imposing tighter restrictions in eligibility requirements for students to qualify for Pell Grants; and,

- constraining the family income eligibility requirements.

Challenges facing current financial aid policy

The following six conditions are some of the challenges facing the national college student aid policy:

(1)   the declining purchasing power of the annual financial aid awards that students receive;

(2)   the shifting balance of federal financial aid awards from grants to loans;

(3)   the unacceptably high default rate on guaranteed loans;

(4)   the minimal effect of financial aid awards on expanding the range of institutions that economically disadvantaged recipients might attend;

(5)   the high drop-out rates of grant recipients before degree program completion; and

(6)   the lack of consideration given to the quality of both college preparation and academic performance in college for determining financial aid eligibility requirements.

Declining purchasing power of financial aid

Among the most formidable challenges to federal financial aid is maintaining its value from year to year. In the ten year period between 1983 and 1994, the average cost of attending America's universities and colleges out-paced the growth rate in federal financial assistance by more than a two-to-one ratio. Figure 2 illustrates that during the past decade the cost in current dollars of attending private four-year universities increased by 94 percent, from

$10,243 to $19,884; at private four-year colleges by 88 percent, from $7,849 to $14,732; at public four-year universities by 76 percent, from $3,899 to $6,862; 74 percent at public four-year colleges, from $3,518 to $6,109; and 44 percent at public two-year colleges, from $2,807 to $4,039. During the same decade Figure 2 shows that the growth in the average Pell Grant increased by 38 percent, from $1,104 to $1,518; the average Stafford Loan increased 33 percent, from $2,297 to $3,061; and the average College Work Study increased 22 percent, from $877 to $1,066 (The College Board, 1994).

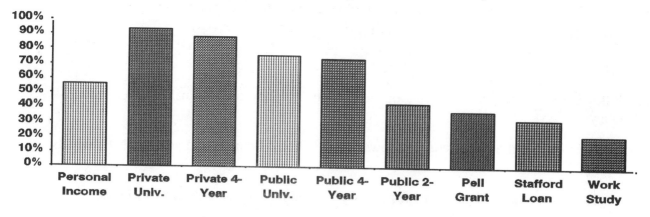

Figure 2
Growth in Personal Income, Average Cost of Attendance, and Federal Financial Aid Awards: 1984-85 to 1993-94 (in current dollars)

From: "Trends in Student Aid: 1984 to 1994," The College Board, Spetember 1994

With the exception of the period between FY 1993 and 1994, when federal appropriations for the Pell Grant program declined by 8 percent, from just over $6 billion to slightly more than $5.5 billion, the Pell Grant program has received annual incremental funding increases for the past decade. The number of recipients during this exceptional year of an 8 percent decrease in appropriations declined from 4.2 million to 3.7 million students, or 12 percent. In addition to the decline in appropriations, more restrictive eligibility requirements may have lead to a decline in student recipients (The College Board, 1994). Despite annual incremental increases in federal appropriations for all other years during the past decade, except the period between 1993 and 1994, the actual maximum award amount in constant 1993 dollars declined from $2,643 in 1983 to $2,263 in 1994. The actual average Pell Grant amount that students received declined in constant 1993 dollars from $1,680 in 1986 to $1,494 in 1994 (The College Board, 1994).

Shift in the balance of loan to grant ratio

Prior to 1980, grants made up over two-thirds of the financial aid awarded by the federal government but, by 1984, grants comprised roughly 29 percent of federal financial aid (excluding College Work-Study) and loans made up the remaining 71 percent. During the past decade, grants continued to lose share of federal aid--going down to 23 percent compared to 77 percent for loans.

High student loan default rates

The National Commission on Responsibilities for Financing Postsecondary Education (1993) reported that in 1991 at least 1 million borrowers defaulted on more than $3 billion in guaranteed student loans. The amount of loans defaulted is approximately 15 percent of the money borrowed. The Commission also reported that 48 percent of students who attended non-degree-granting proprietary institutions and who received a guaranteed student loan defaulted on their repayment compared to 12 percent of the students attending four-year institutions. Interestingly, the National Commission also reported that students with the largest loan indebtedness were least likely to be in default while students with the smallest loan indebtedness were more likely to be in default.

Options for economically disadvantaged students

Complete choice is evidenced by equal attendance rates for various subgroups across institutions of different selectivity and costs of attendance (Dickmeyer, Wessels, & Coldren, 1981; Leslie, 1977). Under this definition, current attendance patterns indicate that lower income individuals do not have equal choice among postsecondary educational institutions. Although dependent undergraduates at all income levels were more likely to be attending four-year than two-year institutions in fall 1989, those with incomes below $30,000 were more likely than students with higher incomes to be attending two-year institutions (NCES, 1993). About 33 percent of dependent undergraduates with incomes between $10,000 and $19,999 were enrolled in public two-year institutions, compared with just 19 percent of those with incomes of $70,000 or more. In contrast, the percent of undergraduates enrolled in four-year doctoral-granting institutions increased with income, ranging from 28 percent of those with incomes less than $10,000 to 50 percent of those with incomes of $70,000 or more. Moreover, although dependent undergraduates at all income levels were more likely to be enrolled in public than private four-year institutions, students with higher incomes were more likely than those with lower incomes to be enrolled in private four-year institutions. Less than 10 percent of dependent undergraduates with incomes under $70,000 were enrolled in private four-year doctoral-granting institutions, compared with 17 percent of those with incomes above $70,000 (NCES, 1993).

Presented here are data on four points. Adequate data on dropouts are not currently available. At present, we know that roughly half of the nation's students who enter college graduate within six years of entry. This dropout rate reflects an inefficiency that colleges and universities are attempting to address. Whether the dropout rate for financial aid recipients differs from that of the overall population is unknown. But, an important question for the research on the national financial aid program is to assess the extent to which national financial aid policy shares this challenge. With respect to the quality of both college preparation and performance in college, the American educational systems are merit-based. In order to make the national financial aid programs compatible with and have common goals with the nation's universities and colleges, it behooves the national financial aid program to include an academic component. In fact, colleges and universities administer much of their financial aid to students on the basis of merit.

The current condition of the national financial aid policy described above leads to questions about what alternative approaches are possible in order not only to preserve but also to improve upon its popular legacy for the future. In order to enhance efficiency, restore credibility, and receive greater benefit from the national policy, the various aid programs will require modifications. Some of the existing programs must be strengthened, some must be replaced with alternative programs, and all programs must be subject to the continuous policy evaluation and research that are needed to monitor and improve the efficiency and effectiveness of the entire national financial aid policy.

Pressure has been mounting upon the national financial aid policy to extend benefits to larger segments of the population (middle class) while simultaneously increasing funding levels to keep pace with inflation for current recipients. The types of pressures currently placed upon the national financial aid policy include the following: (1) increasing student access to college, (2) increasing the rates of student retention and progress through degree programs, (3) reducing the debt burden of students who complete college, (4) permitting highly motivated and academically prepared economically disadvantaged students to attend the nation's best universities for which they are academically qualified, (5) encouraging students to complete higher levels of postsecondary education beyond their first degree (associate's or baccalaureate), and (6) promoting self-help by families to finance their own college education. Recent attempts to patch up the existing policy provide evidence that minor tinkering with how loans are processed, chiseling at the edges of eligibility requirements, raising the per capita amounts provided to students at rates below the growth rates of inflation, and constructing new bureaucracies to chase down fraudulent recipients will not lead to either optimal efficiency or effectiveness of the national financial aid policy.

A reform idea

Reforms in national financial aid policy should address both economic and societal needs and demands for postsecondary education that are not presently being met and encourage more students to enter and persist through completion of college. The national financial aid policy should incorporate the following features that address some of the major challenges to the present policy:

- have the amount of aid keep pace with inflation and the cost of attending college;

- have the amount of aid awards be sufficient to permit financially disadvantaged students to enter and persist in the very best colleges and universities in the nation for which they are academically qualified;

- have financial aid awards give priority to the economically least advantaged students but also give some weight to students' preparation/qualifications for admissions, students' academic performance in college, and students' successful completion of their college degree;

- ensure that the loan programs have minimum default, fraud and abuse in order to make more money available to a greater number of students;

- provide incentives for students to enter and persist through college by using grants to reward economically disadvantaged students for successfully completing their college degree;

- encourage highly qualified students to attend and persist to completion of post-baccalaureate programs; and

- encourage families to save for their children's college expenses.

Rather than adding new programs, the proposed reform advocates major adjustments to realign existing programs, causing them to work in tandem and form a coherent and comprehensive policy. The reform has the following three elements:

- First, students who enter degree programs (associate's, baccalaureate, master's or doctoral) with demonstrated financial need would be awarded subsidized loans to cover all student expenses. If they drop out prior to receiving a degree, then they would begin to repay the loan. All the rules of the existing Stafford Loan Program would apply, except upon successfully completing a degree program, students would qualify for loan forgiveness in the amount of the financial need they exhibited at the time they first entered their degree program. This would be a replacement for existing grant awards (Pell, SEOG, and others) that students presently receive upon entering college;

- Second, rather than eliminating present grant programs, Pell Grants and other need-based federal grants should be reconfigured to be awarded only to students who complete their programs at any of the following degrees levels: associate's, baccalaureate, master's or doctoral;

- Third, an additional grant program would be established to award a fraction of the financial aid grants awarded to students on the basis of their academic performance (grades and progression through the curriculum) as part of the loan forgiveness upon completing their degree programs;

- Fourth, colleges and universities should be offered financial rewards which can be used at their discretion for their own institutional scholarship programs for succeeding in implementing this new national financial aid policy; and

- Fifth, a separate financial aid policy should be established for postsecondary institutions that offer only diplomas and certificates (proprietary institutions). A policy for this sector of postsecondary institutions should be tailored to the unique needs of the students' goals, aspirations, and educational programs. The specific financial aid programs that constitute this policy should be designed to achieve the same efficiencies and effectiveness as those that are being sought in the reform idea expressed in the four previous recommendations.

The details for implementing this approach have yet to be developed and perhaps some experimentation will be required in order to judge the quality and impact. But, this proposed reform has the following potential advantages over the present system of national financial aid:

(1) Grants would be 100 percent effective by ensuring that only students who complete a degree would receive a grant award.

(2) Because grants would be reserved only for college graduates, students would have a disincentive for dropping out, which should in turn help colleges and universities achieve higher retention rates.

(3) Waste in the grants programs would be eliminated because people who do not receive a degree would not have access to grants. These students would have access to loans.

(4) Resources saved in the grant programs could be used to increase the size of the grants awarded to degree recipients, broaden the range of people who receive grants, and extend grant awards to disadvantaged students who receive graduate degrees (master's and doctoral degrees).

(5) Because funding will continue to be available to students attending college in the form of loans, access and opportunity should not be negatively affected.

(6) The financial aid eligibility criteria will include merit in addition to financial need as a vital component.

(7) Each of the programs under the national policy will have a distinct/unique role to play but together will operate as a coherent comprehensive policy.

Questions that need to be addressed

Because this proposed strategy has yet to be implemented, several questions need to be addressed at the point of experimentation or implementation. The important questions include the following:

(1)   What effect does the program have upon students' decisions to enter college and the type of college to which they apply and elect to attend?

(2)   How does the program affect student retention, progression, graduation rates, and academic performance in college?

(3)   How does the program affect student debt burdens and default rates?

(4)   What rewards do colleges and universities merit for succeeding in increasing retention, graduation, and performance of their students?

The proposal advanced in this paper is a novel, yet plausible solution to the stagnation of the existing federal financial aid policy. Perhaps its most compelling dimensions are (1) the inclusion of student performance as a criterion in addition to need in awarding financial aid and (2) the acknowledgment of the importance of extending financial aid in the form of grants and loan forgiveness through the graduate level. Both of these dimensions are important priorities for national economic and social development. In order to further develop this concept, the national government should proceed to invite further refinement of the principle concepts, to develop details for implementation, and to experiment on a modest scale as a first step in national reform.

Michael T. Nettles is professor of education and public policy at the University of Michigan, Ann Arbor. Previously he served as Vice President for Assessment for the University of Tennessee system in Knoxville. Nettles received his Ph.D. in Higher Education from Iowa State University.

References

The College Board (1994). *Trends in Student Aid: 1984 to 1994,* New York.

Dickmeyer, N., Wessels, J., & Coldren, S.L. (1981). *Institutionally Funded Student Financial Aid,* Washington, DC: American Council on Education.

Leslie, L.L. (1977). *Higher Education Opportunity: A Decade of Progress,* Washington, DC: ERIC/Higher Education Research Report, Number 3.

Mortensen, T.G. (1991). Financial Aid Problems for Dependent Students from Low-Income Families, *Journal of Student Financial Aid,* 21 (3), p. 27-38.

Mortensen, T.G. (1990). *The Impact of Increased Loan Utilization Among Low Family Income Students* (ACT Student Financial Aid Research Report Series, Number 90-1). Iowa City: American College Testing Program.

National Commission on Responsibilities for Financing Postsecondary Education (1993). *Making College Affordable Again* (Final Report). Washington, DC.

National Center for Education Statistics (1993). *Financing Undergraduate Education 1990.* U.S. Department of Education, (93-201).

Orfield, G. (1992). Money, Equity, v. College Access. *Harvard Educational Review, 62* (3), p. 337-72.

U.S. Department of Education, National Center for Education Statistics. (1994) *The Digest of Education Statistics, 1994.* Washington, DC: U.S. Government Printing Office.

Participants in the National Conference on Best Ways for the Federal Government to Help Students and Families Finance Postsecondary Education

Dr. Robert Andringa
President
Coalition for Christian
  Colleges and Universities
Washington, DC

Dr. Sandra Baum
Professor and Chair of Economics
Skidmore College
Saratoga Springs, NY

Mr. Stephen Blair
President
Career College Association
Washington, DC

Dr. David Breneman
University Professor and Dean of Education
University of Virginia
Charlottesville, VA

Dr. Patrick Callan
Executive Director
California Higher Education Policy Center
San Jose, CA

Dr. Frederick Capshaw
President
Community College of Philadelphia
Philadelphia, PA

The Honorable Wilhelmina Delco
Chair
National Advisory Committee on
  Institutional Quality and Integrity
Austin, TX

Ms. Janice Dorian
Financial Aid Administrator
Mansfield Beauty Schools
Quincy, MA

Dr. Edward M. Elmendorf
Vice President
Government Relations and Policy
  Analysis
American Association of State
  Colleges and Universities
Washington, DC

Ms. Lynn Fawthrop
Chairperson
Advisory Committee on Student Financial Assistance
Roger Williams University
Bristol, RI

Dr. Conrad Festa
Provost
College of Charleston
Charleston, SC 29424

Dr. Deborah Lee Floyd
President
Prestonsburg Community College
Prestonsburg, KY

Mr. Lawrence Gladieux
Executive Director for Policy
  Analysis
The College Board
Washington, DC

Dr. Gordon Haaland
President
Gettysburg College
Gettysburg, PA

Dr. Terry Hartle
Vice President
Division of Governmental Relations
American Council on Education
Washington, DC

Mr. Arthur Hauptman
Senior Fellow
Association of Governing Boards
  of Universities and Colleges
Washington, DC

Dr. Sam Hayward
Former President
North Carolina State PTA
Raleigh, NC

Ms. Mary Addison Heckerd
President
Student Government Association
College of Charleston
Charleston, SC

Ms. Betsy Hicks
Deputy Assistant Secretary for
  Student Financial Assistance
U.S. Department of Education
Washington, DC

Dr. Stephen Hoenack
Professor of Economics
University of Minnesota
Minneapolis, MN

Dr. Fred Humphries
President
Florida A & M University
Tallahassee, FL

Dr. Richard Ingram
President
Association of Governing Boards
  of Universities and Colleges
Washington, DC

The Honorable Ken Jacobsen
Washington State Representative
Seattle, WA

Mr. Rick Jerue
Counsel for the House Committee on Economic and
  Educational Opportunities
U.S. House of Representatives
Washington, DC

Dr. Bruce Johnstone
Professor
University of Buffalo
Buffalo, NY

The Honorable Nancy Landon Kassebaum
United States Senate
Washington, DC

Mr. Leo Kornfeld
Senior Advisor to the Secretary
U.S. Department of Education
Washington, DC

Ms. Catherine LeBlanc
Executive Director for the
  White House Initiative on
  Historically Black Colleges
  and Universities
U.S. Department of Education
Washington, DC

Dr. Charles Lenth
Director of Policy Studies, Higher Education
Education Commission of the States
Denver, CO

Dr. David Longanecker
Assistant Secretary for
  Postsecondary Education
U.S. Department of Education
Washington, DC

Dr. Dallas Martin
President
National Association of Student
  Financial Aid Administrators
Washington, DC

Dr. Kent McGuire
Program Officer
Pew Charitable Trusts
Philadelphia, PA

Ms. Maureen McLaughlin
Deputy Assistant Secretary for
  Policy, Planning and Innovation
U.S. Department of Education
Washington, DC

Dr. Jim Mingle
Executive Director
State Higher Education Executive
  Officers
Denver, CO

Dr. Peter Mitchell
President
Columbia College
Columbia, SC

Mr. John Morning
Director
Association of Governing Boards
New York, NY

Mr. Mark Musick
President
Southern Regional Education Board
Atlanta, GA

Dr. Michael Nettles
Professor of Education & Public Policy
University of Michigan
Ann Arbor, MI

Dr. Betty J. Overton
Coordinator of Higher Education
W.K. Kellogg Foundation
Battle Creek, MI

Dr. Wayne Patterson
Dean of Graduate Studies
College of Charleston
Charleston, SC

Dr. Terry Peterson
Counselor to the Secretary
U.S. Department of Education
Washington, DC

Dr. David Pierce
President & Chief Executive Officer
American Association of
  Community Colleges
Washington, DC

Dr. Cornelius Pings
President
Association of American Universities
Washington, DC

The Honorable Richard W. Riley
Secretary
U.S. Department of Education
Washington, DC

Mr. Marc Ross
National Association of
  Students for Higher Education
Bowling Green, OH

The Honorable Alexander M. Sanders, Jr.
President
College of Charleston
Charleston, SC

Dr. Ted Sanders
Chancellor
Southern Illinois University
Carbondale, IL

Dr. Robert Scott
Ramapo College of New Jersey
Mahwah, NJ

The Honorable Nikki Setzler
South Carolina State Senate
Columbia, SC

Mr. Fred Sheheen
Commissioner
South Carolina Commission
  on Higher Education
Columbia, SC

Dr. Sue Sommer-Kreese
Vice President for Enrollment
College of Charleston
Charleston, SC

Ms. Clayton Spencer
Chief, Education Counsel (Minority)
Senate Labor and Human Resources Committee
United States Senate
Washington, DC

Dr. Marshall P. Stanton
President
Kansas Wesleyan University
Salina, KS

Mr. Jeff Stesancic
National Association of Students
  for Higher Education
Bowling Green, OH

Dr. Mary Thornley
President
Trident Technical College
Charleston, SC

Dr. Ken Tolo
Senior Advisor, Office of the Secretary
U.S. Department of Education
Washington, DC

Dr. Eleanor Vreeland
Chairman
Katherine Gibbs Schools, Inc.
New York, NY

Dr. David Warren
President & Chief Executive Officer
National Association of
  Independent Colleges and
  Universities
Washington, DC

Dr. Tom Wolanin
Deputy Assistant Secretary for
  Legislation and Congressional
  Affairs
U.S. Department of Education
Washington, DC

THANKS AND SPECIAL ACKNOWLEDGMENTS

Special acknowledgments to people who were instrumental in organizing the conference:

. Senator Nancy Kassebaum for her interest and suggestion that we hold this meeting;

. Terry Peterson, Maureen McLaughlin, Lynn Mahaffie, Karen Wenk, Francine Picoult, Sandy Wood, and Valentina Tikoff of the Department of Education for designing and organizing the conference.

. The Honorable Alexander M. Sanders, Jr., President of the College of Charleston, for hosting the conference;

. Dr. Peter Mitchell and Dr. Mary Thornley, Presidents of Columbia College and Trident Technical College, respectively, for co-sponsoring the conference;

. the paper writers whose ideas served to generate much of the discussion and exchange of ideas;

. all conference participants whose views and perspectives helped shape this publication;

. Elizabeth Kassebaum who coordinated arrangements for the conference at the College of Charleston;

. Kaye Lingle Koonce of Trident Technical College who assisted in organizing the meeting;

. All those who assisted in other ways, including small group facilitators Linda Ketner, Henrietta Franklin, Stephen Bryant, Jeff Dorman, Lisa Dorn Hand; note takers Andy Abrams, W. Hugh Haynsworth, Linda Salane, Judy Everett, Gary Sattelmeyer; and those who taped the conference.

ISBN 0-16-048678-5

90000

9 780160 486784